SPIN-OFF
TO
PAY-OFF

SPIN-OFF TO PAY-OFF

An Analytical Guide to Investing in Corporate Divestitures

Joseph W. Cornell

McGraw-Hill
New York • San Francisco • Washington, D.C. • Auckland
Bogotá • Caracas • Lisbon • London • Madrid • Mexico City
Milan • Montreal • New Delhi • San Juan • Singapore
Sydney • Tokyo • Toronto

Library of Congress Cataloging-in-Publication Data

Cornell, Joseph W., date.
    Spin-off to pay-off : an analytical guide to investing in corporate
divestitures / Joseph W. Cornell.
        p. cm.
    ISBN 0-7863-1204-1
    1. Stocks- -United States.   2. Investments- -United States.
3. Corporate divestiture- -United States.   4. Corporations- -United
States- -Finance.   I. Title.
HG4910.C626 1997
332.63'22'0973- -dc21   97-13945
                                                                           CIP

McGraw-Hill

A Division of The **McGraw·Hill** Companies

    2 3 4 5 6 7 8 9 0 DOC/DOC 9 0 2 1 0 9 8

ISBN 0-7863-1204-1

The sponsoring editor for this book was Steven Sheehan, the editing supervisor
was Donna Namorato, and the production supervisor was Suzanne W. B.
Rapcavage. It was set in Palatino by Lisa M. King of Editorial and Production
Services.

Printed and bound by R. R. Donnelley & Sons Company.

This publication is designed to provide accurate and authoritative information in
regard to the subject matter covered. It is sold with the understanding that
neither the author nor the publisher is engaged in rendering legal, accounting, or
other professional service. If legal advice or other expert assistance is required,
the services of a competent professional person should be sought.

    —*From a Declaration of Principles jointly adopted by a Committee of*
    the American Bar Association and a Committee of Publishers.

This book is printed on recycled, acid-free paper containing a minimum
of 50% recycled de-inked fiber.

To my wife Peggy
and our two wonderful spin-offs

CONTENTS

Chapter 2
Why Spin-Offs Occur   39

Chapter 3
Why Invest in Spin-Offs?   43

Chapter 4
Spin-Offs Are Misvalued   53

Chapter 5
Evaluating Spin-Offs   59

Chapter 6

Timing the Purchase and Sale of the Spin-Off   65

Sell Quickly After the Spin-Off   65
When Should You Invest?   66
  The Pre-Spin Period   66
  The Initial Trading Period   67
  The Seasoning Period   68
  Beware of Buying Too Soon   68

FOR THE RECORD—A LOOK AT THE PAST AND FUTURE

Chapter 7

Completed Spin-Offs   71

Parent	Spin-Off	Spin-Off Date	Page
Adolph Coors Co. (ACCOB)	ACX Technologies (ACTX)	12/21/92	71
Alco Standard Corp. (ASN)	Unisource Worldwide, Inc. (UWW)	1/2/97	72
Allen Group (ALN)	Transpro (TPR)	10/2/95	73
American Express (AXP)	Lehman Brothers (LEH)	5/31/94	75
AMR Corp. (AMR)	Sabre Reservations System (TSG)	10/10/96	75
Anheuser-Busch (BUD)	Earthgrains (EGR)	3/27/96	76
AT&T Corp. (T)	Lucent Technologies (LU)	9/30/96	77
AT&T (T)	NCR (NCR)	1/2/97	78
Ball Corporation (BLL)	Alltrista Corp. (JARS)	4/6/93	79
Baxter International (BAX)	Caremark Int'l (CK)	12/2/92	79
Baxter International (BAX)	Allegiance (AEH)	10/1/96	80
Briggs & Stratton (BGG)	Strattec Security (STRT)	2/28/95	80
Burlington Resources (BR)	El Paso Natural Gas (EPG)	7/1/92	81
Caliber System, Inc. (CBB)	Roadway Express (ROAD)	1/16/96	81

PART THREE

THE FUTURE

Chapter 8
Pending Spin-Offs   149

FOREWORD
Corporate Spin Offs

Nearly a decade ago, I was fresh out of school, hyper-eager, and entirely green behind the ears. I joined a small investment and financial publishing firm in Chicago, ready to cut my teeth on the stock market and blaze a path for myself. Fortunately, Joe Cornell, a fellow teammate and wiser than his years, rescued me from sure self destruction. I started as an analyst/writer, searching for companies with decent growth rates selling at low price-earnings ratios, low debt-to-capital, and a long-term performance record—the standard valuation methodology. But, hell bent on hyperbole, I made screaming buys out of laggard stocks and paned solid growth names. Joe would peruse my writeups and laugh heartily at the gross exaggerations or misrepresentations that I was painting in black and white. So, like everyone, I learned the business the hard way, by making mistakes. To Joe's credit, he was one of the first, along with our boss, to show me several invaluable lessons for reaping stock market profits.

The most important tenet I learned in my rookie year can best be summed up, "Hit 'em where they ain't." Though sounding intuitively basic, if not sophomoric, it's rarely followed. Why? Because human nature often dictates that we need confirmation from others before pursuing a course of action—the so called lemming effect. If an investor sees a stock on the best gainers list that seems attractive, they'll often buy without knowing or researching the fundamentals. Likewise, if that same stock reverses course and begins to fall, indicating others are bailing out, then that investor might sell too—since the fundamentals never drove the buy decision. This whipsawing action leads many investors, professional and individual, to experience sub-par performance. What this book illustrates is one way to take a more reasoned, longer-term and fundamental approach to investing—focused on buying neglected stocks and experiencing gains when other investors recognize their value.

Spin-offs create opportunity through inherent neglect. Let's say XYZ Corporation spins off their Telestar division to shareholders or through a public offering of shares. Rarely are more than two or three brokerage firms involved, so the analyst coverage on the newly public Telestar is severely limited. This leads to a lack of institutional sponsorship: Brokers and analysts are not talking up the Telestar story, so the stock price languishes. This begs the question, then, of why "hit 'em" there if these stocks are languishing? The key is that over time, these sorts of stocks can become big winners. If spun-off companies perform well, then slowly—and surely—investors will take notice. By "hitting them where they ain't," investors can purchase high-quality companies at very reasonable price-earnings multiples and enjoy strong stock performance when the crowds take notice.

So, enjoy the picture that Joe paints. Sharing his experience in this area will not only be profitable for individual and professional investors, but fun as well. When the undiscovered gems he writes about attain prominence, it's a kick to tell your friends at the cocktail party, "Hey, I knew this company before anyone!" Happy Hunting.

Andy Graves
Portfolio Manager
Friess Associates, Inc. Manager of the
Brandywine and Brandywine Blue Funds.

PREFACE

An efficient market is characterized by the inability to earn abnormal returns over the long run. The U.S. capital markets are efficient enough that investment returns above those dictated by the riskiness of the portfolio are very elusive. However, hidden market inefficiencies do exist. Corporate spin-offs are an anomaly that offers a "free-lunch" to improve portfolio returns. This book uncovers the cracks in the efficient market theory which can improve portfolio performance. It discusses how spin-offs can be used by investors to capitalize on excess returns available in a nearly efficient stock market.

Spin-offs often result in a higher aggregate value for the constituent pieces. Many diversified companies are electing to spin-off parts of their business, having found that this form of divestiture leads to greater shareholder value.

Joe Cornell

ACKNOWLEDGMENTS

Many people had a role in bringing this book to fruition. I owe a huge debt of gratitude to my friends Bill Bruggemeier and Joe Seligmann who provided valuable assistance. A special thanks is owed to Jim Moen (AKA, The Velveteen Rabbit, AKA Coco), President of High Yield Analytics, Inc., who gave me encouragement to run with the project as well as the time and support to write this book. Without his friendship, commitment, and patience I would have never been able to complete this project. A big thanks to Steven Sheehan and Kevin Thornton at McGraw-Hill, who believed in this project. Finally, I am grateful to my wife, Peggy, for constantly inspiring me to finish this work on time.

PART **ONE**

AN OVERVIEW
OF CORPORATE
SPIN-OFFS

CHAPTER 1

What Is a Spin-Off?

A spin-off occurs when a company distributes a piece of its corporate assets to the company's existing shareholders in some relation to their existing stock ownership. We will define it as follows:

> *Spin-off: The reorganization of a business in which the original company transfers some of its assets to a newly formed one. The original company receives all of the issued stock of the new company (usually a former subsidiary or division) as consideration in the form of a property dividend on a proportionate basis.*

Since January 1994, more than 100 spin-off transactions have been publicly announced. Many notable companies, such as Sears, AT&T, ITT, GM, Marriott International, Anheuser-Busch, and Kimberly Clark have embraced the spin-off concept in recent years. Why have spin-offs become so popular, and why are they attractive transactions for corporate America?

As we've defined it, a spin-off is a tax-free transaction in which a parent corporation transfers the business to be spun off to a new subsidiary and then pays a special dividend to its shareholders consisting of the shares of the new subsidiary. After a spin-off, the new firm is a separate, publicly traded company with a shareholder base identical to that of the parent corporation. The shareholders of the parent company receive the shares of the subsidiary on a prorata basis, without paying any additional consideration or incurring any tax liability.

3

The foremost advantage of a spin-off is that it is tax efficient. This is especially significant in situations where the assets to be divested have a low cost basis but a high market value. Generally, when a company distributes assets, including subsidiary stock, it recognizes a gain as though it had sold such assets for their fair market value and the recipient shareholder recognizes dividend income on the receipt of the distribution. However, a spin-off that meets the requirements of Section 355 of the Internal Revenue Code is tax-free to the parent corporation and the receiving shareholders.

Spin-offs often help satisfy shareholder demands to unlock hidden value and improve market performance. Institutional investors are increasingly pushing management to increase shareholder value. Many academic studies confirm that spin-offs on average have outperformed the general market (Standard & Poor's 500) by a significant margin. In addition, the evidence suggests a spin-off can improve the market performance of the parent company, too.

From the point of view of the spun-off company, the spin-off can create an opportunity for improved operating performance under a highly focused management team with equity-based incentives. And the spin-off can achieve a market valuation based on its own attributes, unaffected by the businesses of its former parent. A spin-off can offer opportunities for the parent and subsidiary company both that are not available in a typical sale transaction, particularly in cases where the two businesses have disparate operations or capital requirements.

Spin-offs help management successfully facilitate strategic objectives, such as refocusing on "core competencies" or separating leveraged capital intensive businesses from high-growth divisions. Divestitures can remove conflicts of interest between two companies that constrain growth. For example, AT&T spun off Lucent Technologies to enhance that division's ability to sell equipment to AT&T's competitors. Similarly, a spin-off can separate regulated businesses from unregulated businesses, thereby providing greater diversification opportunities.

Spin-offs have gone from being a technique to eliminate poor performers to becoming a means of unlocking value.

1996 was another record year for spin-offs, and there is no sign of a slowdown.

Spin-offs generate greater shareholder value. Many corporate spin-offs offer the potential for above average investment returns.

Over the past several years, spin-off activity has increased notably as corporations have fully or partially divested subsidiaries. In some instances, the stock in the subsidiary is previously sold to the public in an IPO, and the parent uses the spin-off technique to divest itself of remaining subsidiary shares. More often, a market in the subsidiary's stock is produced for the first time once the parent and subsidiary are separated.

One reason for the acceleration in spin-off activity often cited is the belief that the parent or subsidiary is undervalued by the stock market. Many subsidiaries are minor units of large or diversified companies, and management may conclude that either the market ignores the inherent value in the subsidiary by embedding it within the parent, or that the subsidiary detracts from the parent's value. The divestiture forces the market to concentrate on each entity separately. There is sufficient academic evidence to suggest that, on average, returns on spin-off stocks validate the parent company's tactics.[1]

FIGURE 1-1

Breaking Up Is Easy to Do

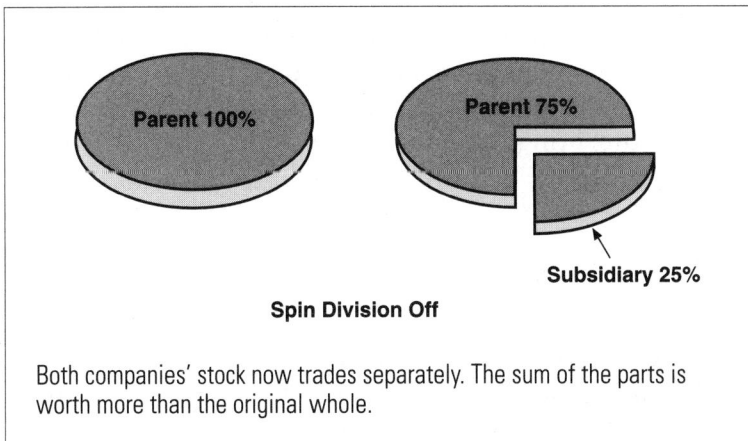

Spin Division Off

Subsidiary 25%

Both companies' stock now trades separately. The sum of the parts is worth more than the original whole.

VARIOUS SPIN-OFF FORMS

The disposition of assets can take one of three broad forms: spin-offs, divestitures, and carve-outs. Spin-offs and carve-outs create new legal entities; divestitures do not. In a spin-off the parent company transfers some of its assets and liabilities to a new firm created for that purpose. The shareholders of the original firm are then given shares in the new firm on a proportional basis to their ownership in the original firm. After the spin-off, the original shareholders have the same equity interest, but it is now divided between two separate entities. The shareholders can choose to sell their stock or keep it. By creating a new firm with its own assets, its own management, and separate ownership, the spin-off represents a real transfer of control.

There are a number of variations on the spin-off, including the split-off. In a split-off, some of the shareholders are given an equity interest in the new firm in exchange for their shares of the parent company. Spin-offs may be and have been described as stock dividends. It is important to note that in all forms of spin-offs the parent company receives no cash from its transfer of assets to the new firm.

An equity carve-out is a form of restructuring that is an intermediate step between a spin-off and a divestiture (an out-and-out sale of assets). It does bring in cash to the original firm but also disperses assets and ownership in the assets to nonowners of the original firm. In a carve-out, the original company forms a new firm and transfers some of the assets to it. The original firm then sells equity in the new firm. The new purchasers of this equity may or may not be the same as the owners of the parents firm. A carve-out, like a divestiture, brings cash to the firm and, like a spin-off, creates a new entity.

The Pure Spin-Off

In a pure spin-off, a parent company distributes 100% of its ownership interests in a subsidiary operation as a dividend to its existing shareholders. The subsidiary has not been

publicly traded prior to the spin-off and is given to its existing shareholder base for no monetary gain. After the spin-off
there are two separate, publicly held firms that have exactly
the same shareholder base. This procedure stands in contrast
to an initial public offering (IPO), in which the parent company is actually selling (rather than giving away) some or all
of its ownership interests in a division. Often, an IPO in which
the parent company retains a majority interest in the new
company may well be a prelude to a spin-off of remaining
interests to existing shareholders.

The "Majority Spin"

In this variant, the parent company spins off the bulk (80 to
90% of the shares) of the subsidiaries' shares. The parent

TABLE 1–1

Major 1995 Spin-Offs

Spun-Off Company	Business	Former Parent	Share Exchange Ratio	Symbol
Castle & Cooke	Real estate	Dole Food Co.	1:3	CCS
Crown Vantage	Specialty paper	James River	1:10	CVAN
Culligan Water	Water purification	Samsonite	1:1	CUL
Darden Restaurants	Restaurants	General Mills	1:1	DRI
Dave & Buster's	Restaurant/club	Edison Brothers	1:5	DANB
Host Marriott Services	Food concessions	Host Marriott Corp.	1:5	HMS
ITT Corp.	Hotels, casinos	ITT Corp.	1:1	ITT
ITT Hartford	Insurance	ITT Corp.	1:1	HIG
ITT Industries	Auto products	ITT Corp.	1:1	IIN
Promus Hotel Corp.	Hotels	Promus	1:2	PRH
Republic Environ- mental	Waste services	Republic Industries	1:1	RESI
Schweitzer-Maduit	Paper products	Kimberly Clark	1:10	SWM
Strattec Security	Auto locks	Briggs & Stratton	1:5	STRT
Transport Holdings	Health insurance	Travelers Group	1:200	TLIC
Transpro	Auto radiators	Allen Group	1:4	TPR
U.S. Industries	Multibusiness	Hanson PLC	1:20	USI

company retains the remaining 10 to 20% to maintain a business, or control, relationship or with the intention of selling its remaining shares at a more favorable future price.

A twist on the majority spin occurs when the parent company actually spins off 100% of the subsidiary shares then outstanding, but retains warrants to purchase the spin-off's stock as part of the spin-off process. A recent example of this method occurred when Bally Entertainment (by now merged with ITT) spun off Bally Fitness (BFIT), on January 9, 1995. Bally Entertainment retained a warrant to purchase 20% of the equity (2.94 shares) exercisable after one year for up to ten years, struck at a price equal to 110% of the average closing price for the first five trading days of Bally Fitness (about $6). For the parent company, the net effect of holding warrants is similar to retaining already existing common shares. The parent company can still expect to profit from any future price appreciation in the spin-off's shares.

The Bally Entertainment spin-off of Bally Total Fitness illustrates many of the benefits that can be achieved in a corporate divestiture. Chicago-based Bally Entertainment Corp. decided in June 1994 to spin-off its fitness-club division to maximize shareholder value. Bally Entertainment, one of the major casino operators in the United States, decided to focus on its more lucrative gaming/resort businesses. In January of 1995, Bally spun off Bally Total Fitness (BFIT) as a dividend to stockholders. Bally Total Fitness is the largest operator of health clubs in the country in terms of revenues, members, and the number of facilities. They run over 300 clubs with more than 4 million members. The purpose of the spin-off was to separate the fast-growing casino/resort businesses from the underperforming health club operations.

What happened? You could have bought the parent company (Bally Entertainment) just prior to the spin-off for around $12 a share, which would entitle you to the Bally Fitness dividend. For every four shares of Bally Entertainment, you would receive one share of Bally Fitness. On January 4, BFIT started trading "when-issued" at $7 and closed the first day of trading at $6.375. The typical selling pressure associated with spun-off firms pushed the stock down below $5. At the present time, Bally Fitness has yet to attract sponsorship from the investment community (still trading around $5) and may be a "sleeper" at current levels. Alternatively, Bally Entertainment has been a home-run. Once separated from the poorly perceived subsidiary, it almost immediately started to trade higher. Within six months of the divestiture, Bally Entertainment agreed to be acquired by Hilton Hotels (this is not unique—very often, companies involved in spin-offs are "picked off" by other firms). Bally's stock traded close to $30 a share before pulling back to $27. Had you bought prior to the spin-off, you would have more than doubled your money in about six months.

EQUITY CARVE-OUTS

In this case, the actual spin-off follows an IPO. A spin-off is sometimes accomplished in two steps. First, the parent corporation sells to the public an interest of less than 20% in the new subsidiary in an Securities and Exchange Commission–registered public offering for cash proceeds. A short time later (usually one to three years), the parent corporation pays a tax-free dividend of the remaining shares of the subsidiary on a prorata basis, without paying any additional consideration or incurring any tax liability. Sears used this two-step technique to divest Allstate Corp. In 1993, Sears sold 19.8% of the common stock outstanding of Allstate in a public offering. In 1995, Sears distributed the remaining 80.2% to Sears' stockholders as a tax-free dividend.

Again, carve-outs involve offering a portion (usually a minority stake) of a subsidiary's stock to the public. Carve-outs are often an intermediate step before a full spin-off is made and are usually a better cash-raising vehicle than a seasoned stock offering made by the parent.

The corporate parent sells a small percentage of a subsidiary's stock to the public in advance of a full spin-off of all the subsidiary's shares to the public. At a later date the remaining shares are spun-off to the parent's existing shareholders. One benefit of this approach is that it establishes a more orderly market for the new company in advance of a full spin-off. Another potential benefit is an increase in the

FIGURE 1–2

Equity Carve-Outs
Parent Sells Equity in the New Firm to the Public (IPO) and Creates a New
Publicly Traded Entity

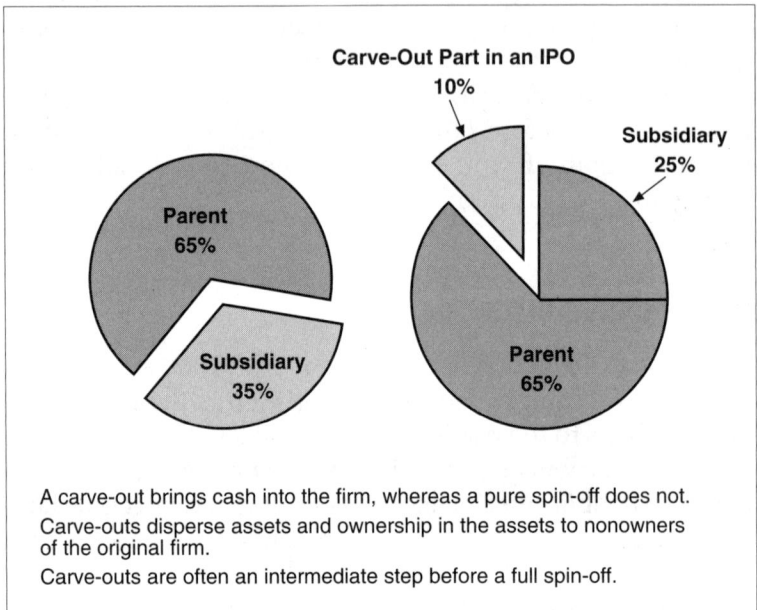

Carve-Out Part in an IPO
10%

Subsidiary
25%

Parent
65%

Subsidiary
35%

Parent
65%

A carve-out brings cash into the firm, whereas a pure spin-off does not.
Carve-outs disperse assets and ownership in the assets to nonowners
of the original firm.
Carve-outs are often an intermediate step before a full spin-off.

parent's stock price that results from highlighting its internal asset values. Then again, the parent might just want to use the cash generated for other corporate purposes. Carve-outs may also provide an efficient way for subsidiaries to raise capital. This can be useful in that if the parent's credit situation may not warrant or attract capital, the subsidiary's investment appeal might. In addition, carve-outs help align management's objectives with those of the new public entity, which can improve operating performance.

This is the strategy that AT&T used when they divested Lucent Technologies, the telecom equipment company, as part of AT&T's historic "trivestiture" restructuring. Following its formation, Lucent was launched as an entity independent from the four systems and technology businesses of AT&T along with the majority of Bell Labs. AT&T offered 18% of Lucent to the public on April 3, 1996, in a $3 billion IPO of

112 million shares at $27. In Fall 1996, AT&T emancipated the balance of Lucent to AT&T shareholders in a tax-free spin-off. Lucent Technologies is one of the world's leading manufacturers and marketers of telecommunications equipment, software, and network integration services, serving 23 of the world's top 25 telecom network operators, selling to more than 90% of the Fortune 500 companies, and number one in sales of North American wireless infrastructure, domestic PBXs, voice processing systems, and domestic consumer telephone products. Roughly one-quarter of the company's sales come from abroad.

Lucent should enjoy faster than historical revenue growth after being liberated from AT&T's communication businesses. Lucent traditionally has done little business with Sprint and none with MCI, since those carriers have long competed with AT&T for long-distance market share. Clearly Lucent's ability to pursue business is enhanced by its being separated from AT&T. Another conflict resolved by the spin-off was that waged between Lucent and AT&T's other businesses over financial and other corporate resources. As an independent entity, Lucent can make its own investment and capital decisions.

1995 CARVE-OUTS IN DETAIL

Amerigas Partners, L.P. (APU) commenced operations on April 19, 1995 as the nation's largest retail propane marketer. APU completed an initial public offering of 17.6 million common units at a price of $21.25 per unit, representing 42% ownership. UGI Corporation (UGI), through its subsidiaries, owns the remaining 58%. APU serves more than 935,000 customers in 44 states. The partnership operates an extensive storage and distribution network, using pipelines, barges, rail cars, and tanker trucks to transport propane to its 580 local market distribution locations. The partnership's operations are managed by its general partner AmeriGas Propane, Inc., a wholly owned subsidiary of UGI. UGI is a 113-year-old supplier of natural gas and other energy services. The units of the partnership have traded in a tight range of a few dollars since carved out of UGI.

TABLE 1–2

Equity Carve-Outs, 1995

Company	IPO Date	IPO Price	Price 12/31/96	% Change
Amerigas Partners LP (propane) Parent: UGI Corp.	4/12/95	21 ¼	22 ⅜	+53%
Ascent Entertainment Group Inc. (TV, radio, sports teams) Parent: COMSAT Corp.	12/13/95	15	15	0%
Boise Cascade Office Products Corp. (Office supplies) Parent: Boise Cascade	4/6/95	12 ½	20 ¾	+83%
Computer Learning Centers (Computer training) Parent: General Atlantic Corp.	7/6/95	8	28 ½	+256%
Congoleum Corp. (Vinyl floor products) Parents: American Biltrite	2/1/95	13	13 ⅞	+6.7%
Donaldson, Lufkin & Jenrette Inc. (Investment banking) Parent: Equitable Cos.	10/25/95	27	36	+33%
HCIA Inc. (Information systems) Parent: Ambac Inc.	2/22/95	14	34 ½	+146%
Hospitality Properties Trust (REITs) Parent: Health and Property Trust	8/16/95	25	29	+16%
Integrated Measurement Systems Inc. (Measurement software) Parent: Cadence Design Systems Inc.	7/20/95	11	17 ⅜	+58%
Intimate Brands Inc. (Retailing) Parent: The Limited Inc.	10/23/95	17	17 ⅛	0%
Nabisco Holdings Inc. (Food) Parent: RJR Nabisco	1/19/95	24 ½	38 ⅞	+59%
Palmer Wireless Inc. (Telecommunications) Parent: Palmer Communications	3/14/95	14 ¼	10 ½	-26%
Shared Technologies Cellular Inc. (Cellular phone service) Parent: Shared Technologies Corp.	4/21/95	5 ¼	1 ¾	-67%

TABLE 1–2

(Continued)

Company	IPO Date	IPO Price	Price 12/31/96	% Change
ThermoSpectra Corp. (Precision imaging instruments) Parent: Thermo Instrument Corp.	8/3/95	14	12 ¼	-12.5%
Toy Biz Inc. (Toys) Parent: Marvel Entertainment Corp.	2/23/95	18	19 ½	+8.3%

Ascent Entertainment (GOAL) is a diversified entertainment and media company that operates production and distribution businesses of well-known franchises. COMSAT carved out about 17% of Ascent in a December 1995 IPO at $15 a share. It provides on-demand in-room video entertainment services to the lodging industry through its 85% owned subsidiary, On-Command Video Corporation (OCV). The company also provides satellite-distribution support services to affiliates of the NBC television network through its wholly owned subsidiary, Ascent Network Services, Inc. It also owns the Denver Nuggets basketball franchise and the Colorado Avalanche hockey franchise, as well as the Beacon Communications television production company. In October 1996, Comsat announced plans to divest its 80% ownership interest in Ascent Entertainment through a sale, spin-off, or other transaction. Comsat said Ascent's need for capital to fund growth was constraining the company's balance sheet and its ability to expand its core telecommunications business.

Boise Cascade Office Products (BOP), based in Itasca, Illinois, is one of the world's largest distributors of office supplies, office furniture, and other office products directly to large corporate, government, and other offices as well as to home offices and small and medium-sized businesses through its direct-marketing channel. The company distributes a broad line of over 11,000 branded and private label products for use in the office.

BOP was operated as the Boise Cascade Office Products Division of Boise Cascade until its IPO at $12.50 (split adjusted), on April 7, 1995. After the offering BCC owned 82.7% of the company's common stock.

Computer Learning Centers (CLCX) operates a chain of 12 for-profit schools that provide adults with training in computer and information technology (IT). Through its accredited programs, the company offers Associate Degree and nondegree diplomas in four primary areas of study, including business applications, electronic systems and hardware, programming, and networking. Job placement rates for graduates of its training programs (a key selling point to potential students) are roughly 85%. It has designed its training programs and courses to focus on current technology needs, offering instruction in fast-growing areas such as client-server environment, networking, and object-oriented programming. Given the demand for computer-literate employees, growth prospects are good for CLCX. The company is projected to generate roughly $60 million in sales for the year (ending January 1997) and approximately $1 per share in earnings.

CLXC, formally a subsidiary of General Atlantic Corporation, completed an initial public offering on July 6, 1995 at $8 per share. CLCX's price hit a high of $33 in Fall 1996 for a stunning 400% increase from the IPO price. But there is a potential crimp in CLCX's business—high student loan default rates, which can spell big trouble for the company. When default rates rise above 25%, funds available to students under Title IV federal aid programs can be withdrawn. Computer Learning Centers gets most of its revenues from such aid, about 72% in fiscal 1996. In fact, the company's Chicago and Philadelphia schools recently received notifications from the Department of Education that CLCX lost its Title IV loan eligibility for Chicago for two loan programs (FFEL & Pell grants), which provided 70% of Chicago's tuition revenue. This will have a negative impact on sales and earnings for the company.

After an October 1996 secondary offering, General Atlantic still retains a 25% equity stake in the company. The company has 5 million shares outstanding for a current market capitalization of about $150 million.

Congoleum (CGM) is North America's second largest manufacturer of resilient vinyl flooring, serving both commercial and residential markets with products. CGM's products are used primarily by the remodeling, replacement, commercial, manufactured home, and new residential markets. The Congoleum brand has been associated with the flooring industry since 1924. The company completed its initial public offering in February 1996, placing 4.7 million shares at $13 a share. Congoleum is a 44% owned subsidiary of American Biltrite (AMEX: ABL).

Donaldson, Lufkin & Jenrette (DLJ) is a leading investment banking firm that serves institutional, corporate, governmental, and individual clients. DLG's businesses include securities underwriting, sales and trading, investment banking, financial advisory services, investment research, correspondent brokerage services, on-line investment services, and asset management. Founded in 1959 and headquartered in New York City, DLJ employs 5,700 individuals worldwide and maintains offices in 12 cities in the United States and 11 cities in Europe, Latin America, Africa, and Asia.

Approximately 80% of the outstanding shares of common stock of DLJ are beneficially owned by The Equitable Companies Incorporated (NYSE: EQ). DLJ went public for the second time in 25 years in October 1995, when it was carved out of The Equitable Companies (Equitable bought the company 10 years ago). In the October public offering, a total of 10.58 million shares were sold at $27 per share. DLJ itself raised $89.1 million from the sale of 3.3 million primary shares to the public. The Equitable sold 7.28 million secondary shares, reducing its ownership interest to 80%.

HCIA, Inc. (HCIA) is a healthcare information company that markets clinical and financial decision-support products to hospitals, integrated delivery systems, managed care organizations, and pharmaceutical manufacturers. The company's databases and products are used to benchmark clinical performance and outcomes and to manage the cost and delivery of healthcare. The company's products range from standardized databases to highly focused systems that assist its customers in evaluating the efficacy and economics of healthcare. HCIA's customers include hospitals, integrated delivery systems, pharmaceutical and medical supply companies, and managed care organizations.

Baltimore-based HCIA was founded in 1985 and went public on February 22, 1995, completing an IPO of 2 million shares at $14 per share as a carve-out of AMBAC (a New York–based holding company that provides insurance and financial services). The stock has traded from a low of 17 $\frac{5}{8}$ to a high of 66 $\frac{3}{8}$. In April 1996, AMBAC sold its remaining interest in HCIA at a price of $51 a share. HCIA proved to be an excellent investment. The move from an IPO price of $14 a share to a peak price of $66 some 17 months later (July 1996) represented a maximum return of 370%.

Hospitality Properties Trust (HPT) is a real estate investment trust (REIT). The company invests in income-producing properties, particularly full-service, limited service, and extended stay hotels. The company owns 37 Courtyard by Marriott hotels. The company completed its initial public offering on August 22, 1995. The company was a 100%-owned subsidiary of Health and Retirement Properties Trust (HRP), which remains an affiliate. Headquartered in Newton, Massachusetts, it invests in hotels leased to unaffiliated hotel operating companies and has investments and commitments of approximately $857 million in 83 hotels in 27 states. HPT pays out $2.36 per share per year in dividends. The REIT has traded in a tight range of $25 to $28 a share since the carve-out.

Integrated Measurements Systems, Inc. (IMS) was founded in 1983 to design and develop engineering test systems to test and measure complex electronic devices at the prototype stage. The company was independent until it was acquired by Valid Logic in 1989. In 1991, Valid Logic merged with Cadence Design Systems, Inc. Both Logic and Cadence operated IMS as a separate company. In July 1995, the company completed an initial public offering of common stock at $11 per share, yielding net proceeds to the company and Cadence of $3.3 million and $26.6 million respectively. Following the IPO, Cadence owns 55% of the stock, with the remaining 45% publicly owned and traded. The carve-out was motivated by IMS's desire to work with Cadence competitors such as Mentor Graphics and Synopsis.

Beaverton, Oregon–based Integrated Measurement Systems, Inc. sells chipmaker's test equipment and software to catch errors early in the engineering cycle. IMS' test stations come into play after chipmakers use software tools to design circuits. Flaws in chip designs are costly, so engineers are hard-pressed to test and evaluate them. IMS' test machines cost between $200,000 and $1.2 million. The company has sold more than 800 systems—about a third of those in foreign markets. The company's test stations focus on complicated chip designs that provide higher margins, rather than "commoditylike" memory chips. Sales grew 37% to $41 million in 1995. Intel is IMS's biggest customer representing 30% of sales in 1995.

Intimate Brands Inc. (IBI) is a specialty retailer of intimate apparel and personal-care products, operating primarily under its Victoria's Secret and Bath & Body Works brand names. Victoria's Secret is the most successful brand of lingerie in the world. More than 560 shops showcase an indulgent collection of intimate apparel, sleepwear, fine fragrances, body care products, and gifts. Bath & Body Works sells personal-care products for people who are concerned about the environment. The business was launched in September 1990 to provide a complete line of products using effective formulations and natural ingredients.

IBI was carved out of The Limited, Inc., a leading specialty retailer that offers a diverse array of women's, men's, and girls' fashion clothing and personal care products through 12 retail divisions and one mail-order operation. On

October 24, 1995, the divisions comprising IBI—Victoria's Secret Stores, Victoria's Secret Catalogue, Bath & Body Works, Cacique, Penhaligon's, and Gryphon—became a separate, NYSE-traded company. Management at The Limited felt that carving out IBI would make the division directly accountable to shareholders by establishing a direct, clear link between performance and shareholder value. The Limited owns approximately 83% of Intimate Brands Inc.

Palmer Wireless (PWIR) constructs and operates cellular-telephone systems and provides cellular-telephone services to over 200,000 subscribers in Alabama, Florida, South Carolina, and Georgia. The company also sells its service and cellular telephones and related accessories though its network of retail stores. PWIR markets all of its products under the Cellular One brand name. The stock is off 26% from its IPO price of $14 ¼ in March of 1995.

Shared Technologies Cellular (STCL), based in Wethersfield, Connecticut, is the nation's leading provider of cellular telephone rental services. Through marketing agreements with Hertz, Avis, National, and Budget car rental companies, United Airlines, Continental Airlines, Delta Shuttle, major hotels, and a national, toll-free reservation number, travelers can rent portable phones and debit (prepaid) cellular phone management systems. The company also doles out phones at conventions, disasters, and special events (the company rented more than 1,700 cellular phones at the 1996 Olympic Games in Atlanta). Since the IPO in April 1995, the company has bought out several rivals, and more acquisitions are likely. Besides renting, the company activates cell phones nationwide, in effect making them "live" for carriers and retailers. The company also offers prepaid debit phones for people with low credit ratings and manages cellular systems for corporations. The thinly traded stock completed its initial pubic offering in April 1995, selling 950,000 shares of its common stock at $5.25 per share. As of December 31, 1995, STCL was approximately 59% owned by Shared Technologies. Subsequent to the issuance of a Series A Preferred Stock, Shared Technologies voting control of the company decreased to approximately 40%. The stock has dropped precipitously since the IPO to $1 ¾ per share, as the company has diluted the stock for additional financing.

Shared Technologies (STCH) (the parent company), provides shared telecommunications services in 488 buildings in 35 cities across the United States. On March 13, 1996, Shared Technologies announced its acquisition of Fairchild Communications Systems, the shared tenant-services arm of the Fairchild Corporation, for about $304 million. At that time the company changed its name to Shared Technologies Fairchild, Inc. The company is now the largest provider of shared telecommunications services in the United States. It provides shared telecommunications systems and services to commercial tenants in office buildings in which STCH typically installs a PBX switch under exclusive agreements with building owners, thereby permitting customers to obtain all their telecommunication needs from a single point of contact.

ThermoSpectra Corp. (THS) makes precision-imaging, inspection, and measurement instruments. The company's products include digital oscillographic recorders that analyze brain and heart activity, digital storage oscilloscopes that record and analyze automobile airbag-inflation specifications, and x-ray inspection systems that screen printed circuit boards for defects. Thermo Instruments (the parent company) still owns 72% of THS.

Toy Biz Inc. (TBZ), founded in 1988, distributes toys as a licensee of Marvel Entertainment Group and other companies and markets its own toy line. Toy Biz and Marvel got together in 1993, when Toy Biz decided to swap 46% of its equity with Marvel in exchange for a perpetual, royalty-free license for the 3,500 Marvel comic book characters. About half of Toy Biz's revenues are derived from Marvel-related toys. Currently, Fox Children's network run X-Men and the Incredible Hulk cartoons and will introduce at least four new Marvel cartoons over the next seven years, each tantamount to a half-hour infomercial for Toy Biz products. The company has achieved significant growth since 1991. Its net sales more than quadrupled, growing from approximately $45.1 million in 1991 to approximately $196.4 million in 1995. This growth has been driven by the sales of action-figure toys based on the Marvel characters and, more recently, by sales of Toy Biz's proprietary dolls and activity toys.

On November 20, 1996, Andrews Group announced a proposal to acquire all outstanding shares of Toy Biz Class A Common Stock. On December 16, 1996, Toy Biz agreed to endorse a transaction under which Andrews Group will acquire all shares of Toy Biz Class A common stock held by shareholders at a price of $22.50 per share. Andrews Group has proposed that it also acquire additional shares of Marvel Entertainment (NYSE: MRV) common stock from Marvel and that Toy Biz become a wholly owned subsidiary of Marvel. The deal for Toy Biz is conditional upon the consummation of the Andrews Group investment in Marvel and the execution of definitive documentation with Toy Biz.

In February 1995, Toy Biz completed an IPO of 2.75 million shares of class A common stock at $18 per share.

Divestiture IPOs

Another form of an equity carve-out is known as a divestiture IPO. Divesting a subsidiary by selling all or most of its shares to the public is a relatively uncommon technique for restructuring companies with varied businesses. There are considerable costs associated with bringing a subsidiary public. The time and resources required in getting an IPO filed with the Securities and Exchange Commission, conducting road shows for investors, and ensuring that the unit is viable on its own. It is not surprising many companies decide to sell the unwanted business outright for cash, or as indicated by the recent rise in spin-offs, give it to its own shareholders. But the strong performance of divestiture IPOs in recent years could cause restructuring firms to consider divestiture IPOs as an alternative format.

Table 1-3 shows some well-known divestiture IPOs from 1995 and their performance measured to December 31, 1996. The selling company retained an interest of one third or less.

TABLE 1–3

Divestiture IPOs from 1995

Company	IPO Date	IPO Price	Price 12/31/96	% Change
Borders Group Inc. (Bookstores) Parent: Kmart Corp.	5/24/95	14 ½	35 ⅞	+147%
Investors Financial Services Corp.* (Administration services) Parent: Eaton & Vance	11/11/95	16 ½	27 ¾	+68%
Midwest Express Holdings, Inc. (Airline) Parent: Kimberly Clark	9/21/95	18	36	+100%
PMI Group Inc. (Mortgage insurance) Parent: Allstate Corp.	4/10/95	34	55 ⅜	+63%

*The remainder of the shares were spun-off after the IPO.

SPLIT-OFFS

By now you know the old-fashioned, pure spin-off essentially gave investors a share in a new firm while they retained shares in the parent. In a split-off, the investor must decide between the new company and the parent. Each shareholder must make a choice: does he or she want to continue owning stock in the old parent or, instead, give up some or all ownership of it in order to get a portion of a new firm containing assets that the parent wants to shed? The split-off technique has been utilized more in the last couple of years. Some of the companies that have divested subsidiaries in this fashion are Eli Lilly, Cooper Industries, Price/Costco, and GM.

To see how this works in practice, assume that a parent

company wants to divest a subsidiary. It would offer its existing shareholders stock in the subsidiary in exchange for shares in the parent company. If the parent distributes 80% of the subsidiary's stock, the divestiture is tax-free. What's more, in an effort to induce enough shareholders to swap stock, investors are offered shares in the subsidiary that are worth more than the shares being returned to the parent company. This offered "premium" is tantamount to free money and explains why split-offs are often oversubscribed. For shareholders, a split-off can be perfect, assuming they have a strong preference for certain businesses of the parent company.

Two companies that were separated from their parents in split-offs in 1995 have proven to be big winners. Guidant, a medical-devices firm separated from Eli Lilly in September 1995, has doubled in price. And the shares of Cooper Cameron, an oil service and equipment maker, have tripled since it was shed by Cooper Industries in July 1995.

Cooper Industries (NYSE: CBE) decided to get out of the oil services businesses it had acquired over the years. In September 1994, they announced their intention to split-off Cooper Cameron, their industrial oil and gas equipment division. Then they invited shareholders who wished to own oil field services assets to tender their shares to Cooper Industries for shares of Cooper Cameron (NYSE: RON). Cooper shareholders where offered the opportunity to exchange 9.5 million Cooper Industries for RON shares. The split-off (exchange) ratio was 2.25:1. The offer was heavily oversubscribed. People who were savvy enough to take a stake in Cooper Cameron were well rewarded, as the shares have roughly quadrupled since the divestiture.

I assure you the choice to swap CBE shares for RON was not obvious to most shareholders. Over the previous four years, RON had been one of the worst, if not the worst, performing companies in the energy services industry. It had seen revenues decline 30% and operating revenue fall 97%. Astute shareholders believed that the characteristics for a turnaround (which panned out) where in place: (1) RON had excellent product lines, but poor marketing and sales; (2) CBE had invested heavily in RON's asset base, but there was too much capacity; (3) RON's cost structure was bloated and inefficient; (4) RON's previous financial goals were focused on contributing to CBE's earnings per share at all costs, rather than maximizing the cash flow and value of the entity; and (5) the markets for the company's products had bottomed and where improving. The split-off acted as the primary catalyst in the turnaround. Management unshackled from CBE focused the company in the right direction and successfully executed a turnaround that drastically improved operating and financial performance.

Eli Lilly successfully split-off Guidant, after it first made a public offering of some Guidant shares in December 1994 (a carve-out) to establish a value for the medical devices operation. For the split-off, Lilly offered its shareholders 3.49 shares of Guidant for each share of Lilly the parent took back. When the offer was announced (August 1995), Guidant's stock sold for about $25, while Lilly stock traded for around $77 per share. Therefore, according to the exchange ratio, one share of Lilly was then worth $86 of Guidant stock—almost a 12% premium. You did not have to be an arbitrageur to surmise it would be advantageous to tender your Lilly stock. Lilly found that the exchange offer was a bit too generous, as it was oversubscribed by a factor of three and had to be awarded pro rata. Because investor demand for Guidant shares outstripped supply of the shares, Lilly took back only 34% of the stock offered by each investor who wanted to swap 100 shares or more.

This illustrates the finesse required by the parent company in setting the terms of the exchange offer in a split-off. The parent wishes to set the exchange ratio so that just enough shareholders want the new subsidiary. If the exchange offer is too stingy, the split-off shares will have no takers. If it is too charitable, then all of the parent's shareholders will rush to participate, and the shares will have to be allocated pro rata.

From the parent's point of view there isn't any major difference between a split-off and a spin-off. Either way the firm rids itself of a disparate asset without incurring a corporate capital gains tax. When the dust settles, the split-off leaves the parent with somewhat fewer shares outstanding. It is akin to a stock buyback without using cash. The success of the Cooper Cameron and Guidant split-offs will likely drive further use of this divestiture technique.

MORRIS TRUST TRANSACTIONS

The Morris Trust transaction represents one of the better planning opportunities in the world of corporate taxes. The transaction, named after a court case lost by the IRS many years ago, not only effectively allows shareholders to dispose of their stock following a spin-off (otherwise prohibited by the device and continuity rules) but makes that very disposition the business purpose for the spin-off.

The Morris Trust structure typically is used when an acquirer, ordinarily a public company, wishes to merge with another firm but wants only part of the target's operations. To divest the unwanted businesses, the target spins-off a subsidiary to its shareholders and immediately merges with the acquirer in a tax-free reorganization. It is usually necessary for the merger to be entirely tax-free to the target shareholders, and no cash is permitted in the transaction.

Morris Trust deals have been under attack. The Clinton administration has proposed legislation to eliminate tax benefits for Morris Trust-type spin-offs. The bill would impose taxes where none now exist and establish a high hurdle that a Morris Trust deal must clear to remain tax-free. In the past, the Morris Trust format has allowed an acquirer to virtually pick and choose the parts of a target company it wants while evading taxes liabilities. Typically, the target spins-off the unwanted operations to stockholders as a separate company and sells the remaining core to the buyer.

The administration's proposal would continue tax-free treatment only for Morris Trust deals in which shareholders of the target company own more than 50% of both companies, unlikely when companies are invariably much larger than their targets. If that criterion cannot be met, capital gains taxes would be levied on both the parent corporation and the individuals receiving shares of the spun-off company.

There has been a flurry of these types of transactions as

companies have rushed to slide in Morris Trust deals before the proposal becomes law.

TARGETED STOCK

As the name implies, companies create these stocks to track the fortunes of one or more of their subsidiaries. Companies often feel that Wall Street analysts and investors incorrectly value subsidiaries that are overshadowed by the parent. So investment bankers tell them that the creation of a tracking stock, also known as a targeted or letter stock, creates "pure plays" that can be valued higher by the market. The unit's finances are reported independently of the parent. Thus, theoretically, if the subsidiary's profits soar, so should the value of the targeted stock. Targeted stocks have some advantages over spin-offs. Issuing tracking stocks is always a tax-free procedure, and if either of the two units is losing money, the earnings of one would offset the losses of the other for tax purposes. Borrowing costs for the unit usually are lower because it relies on its parent's higher credit rating. Overhead costs are lower than if the two were separate. And if there are synergies between the parent and the subsidiary there are added benefits.

As with spin-offs, the biggest reason for issuing targeted stock is the potential to bump up the parent's stock price. Often the company is followed by one group of analysts who understand the business of the parent but not that of the subsidiary. Creating a targeted or tracking stock may prompt separate analyst coverage of the unit, thereby enticing new sponsorship for the company.

History of Targeted Stock

Targeted stock has been used for value enhancement and equity-market focus by USX Corporation and the Pittston Company. Targeted stock structures also were used for acquisitions such as General Motors' purchases of Electronic Data Systems and Hughes Electronics. Targeted stock traces its roots to 1984, when General Motors Corp. created the first security of this type, Class E common stock, to separately reflect its EDS subsidiary. The Class E stock was used to help GM fund the acquisition of EDS, which traded at much higher multiples than GM. EDS leapt sevenfold from the time General Motors Corp. acquired the computer services company in 1984 until the unit was spun off in 1996. In 1985, GM issued another class of common stock (Class H) to fund its acquisition of Hughes Aircraft. In 1991, USX Corporation created targeted stocks for its Marathon Group and U.S. Steel Group, and in 1992 did the same for its Delphi business.

The Mechanics

Targeted stock is a special class of common stock whose return to investors is linked to the performance of a specific group of assets within the company. This "targeting" offers investors more clearly defined and simplified choices by grouping assets with similar investment characteristics and is designed to provide a return to equity investors linked to the performance of a particular business unit, the targeted business. The value of the targeted business is based on the operating performance of its underlying targeted business and is affected by the same factors as regular common stock (earnings, dividends, assets, relative valuations, etc.).

A targeted stock is created when a company authorizes a new class of its common stock and designates the targeted business for that stock. The existing common stock is redesigned to reflect the performance of the remaining businesses; thus, a minimum of two targeted stocks is created in any such transaction. Unlike a spin-off, no legal separation of the assets or liabilities is required. The company continues to borrow as a consolidated entity and leverage the strength of the consolidated assets. Additionally, there is no change in tax posture or board structure. As a result, holders of targeted stock are also shareholders in the company, not the underlying targeted business.

In theory, targeted stocks can provide expanded research coverage, increased shareholder value, and more attractive incentive plans for management. The "pure plays" formed by targeted stock may attract new investors and lead to a more efficiently valued company.

Targeted Stock Attributes

- Targeted stock involves no legal separation of the company. The targeted business remains a part of the consolidated company. Although a company's assets and liabilities are attributed to the targeted groups, the issuance of targeted stock does not affect legal title to such assets or responsibility for such liabilities.

- Targeted stock represents common stock interests in the company, not direct ownership interests in the targeted business. This is relevant in terms of voting rights, EPS calculations, and so forth.

- Separate financial statements for each targeted business are prepared in accordance with generally accepted accounting principles (GAAP). The financial statements for a targeted business are presented to holders of the corresponding targeted stock along with the consolidated financial of the company.

Objectives of Restructuring via Targeted Stock

Targeted stock can be an effective restructuring alternative. Targeted stock enables a more appropriate market valuation by creating a pseudo pure play, thereby increasing access to equity investors. Targeted stock allows for continued access to credit markets as a consolidated entity, thereby maintaining the access to fixed income investors that a larger company provides. Debt investors prefer the reduced volatility of earnings and cash flow potential from a diversified enterprise. While equity investors often discount a conglomerate, debt investors benefit from it. Under targeted stock, a company's credit rating continues to be based on the consolidated entity, and debtholders retain the ability to lay claim to all of the assets and earnings of the consolidated entity.

Benefits of Targeted Stock

- Provides investors a choice.
- Enhances appropriate value recognition on a continuing basis.
- Retains strategic benefits at a combined entity.
- Enhances financial flexibility.
- Facilitates greater operating focus, incentive alignment, and financial accountability.

TABLE 1–4

Targeted Stocks

Issuer	Security	Date of Issuance
General Motors Corporation	Automotive (GM)	Sept. 1984
Electronic Data Systems (GME)*		Sept. 1984
Hughes Electronics (GMH)		Oct. 1985
USX Corporation	U.S. Steel Group (X)	May 1991
	Marathon Group (MRO)	May 1991
	Delphi Group (DGP)	Sept. 1992
The Pittston Company	Services Group (PZS)	July 1993
	Minerals Group (PZM)	July 1993
Ralston Purina Company	Ralston Purina Group (RAL)	July 1993
	Continental Baking (CBG)**	July 1993
Fletcher Challenge Ltd. ADR	Forests Division (FFS)	Nov. 1993
	Ordinary Division (FLC)	Nov. 1993
Genzyme Corporation	General Division (GENZ)	Dec. 1994
	Tissue Repair Div. (GENZL)	Dec. 1994
US West	US West Commun. (USW)	Nov. 1995
	US West Media Group (UMG)	Nov. 1995
Pittston Services Group	Pittston Brink's Group(PZB)	Jan. 1996
	Pittston Burlington (PZX)	Jan. 1996

*On June 10, 1996, General Motors Corp. split-off Electronic Data Systems. Under terms of the tax-free deal, each share of Class E stock was exchanged for one share of the new EDS common stock. EDS common started trading on the New York Stock Exchange on June 10.. The split-off brings to a close GM's dozen years of ownership of EDS, which it bought from Texas billionaire Ross Perot in 1984 for $2.5 billion.

**Continental Baking Group was "called" back by Ralston Purina and in July 1995 sold the business to Interstate Baking.

Example of a Targeted Stock

In April 1995, US West revealed its plan to create targeted stocks. The plan created two new classes of stock: one reflecting the company's 14 state telecommunications business, and another representing its multimedia businesses. The restructuring was engaged to enhance value recognition and financial flexibility. "This method of recapitalizing our business allows us to continue catering synergies between groups, while enabling investors to identify which parts of our business are most attractive to them," said US West Chairman and CEO Richard McCormick.

The plan was implemented through a tax-free distribution that allowed shareholders to continue holding the same level of economic interest in the company. Owners of US West Inc. stock on the record date received, on a tax-free basis, a new share of US West Media Group for every share of US West owned. The US West Media Group shares reflect the performance of US West's cable, wireless, and content interests. The performance of both US West and US West Media Group have lagged the market significantly.

DO INVESTORS PREFER SPIN-OFFS OVER TRACKING STOCKS?

The jury is still out on tracking stocks. For every EDS, which appreciated 700% since being issued by GM in 1984, there is a USX Corp. or US West Communications Group whose tracking stocks have been stuck in neutral. Companies choosing to issue tracking stocks seem to want to have their cake and eat it too. The rub with targeted stocks is that they're not separate companies. Holders of the tracking stock do not actually own the subsidiary. The creation of a tracking stock offers no promise of new management or additional wealth for the holders. Certainly the potential for conflict of interest is present; for example, if the parent gets into financial straits, it could drain resources of the subsidiary to prop itself up. Conflicts may arise in overlapping businesses that want to go after the same contract or customer. The biggest drawback with tracking stocks is that they are essentially immune from takeovers because they are still subsidiaries. Spinning-off the unit seems to be a better idea if the company is truly interested in creating shareholder wealth.

Circuit City (NYSE: CC) recently announced (11/1/96) a plan to create two series of common stock to track the separate performance of its Circuit City and CarMax retail businesses. The plan will create two tracking stocks in Circuit City Stores, Inc. One stock will reflect the performance of the used and new car retail business, which will be designated as the CarMax Group. The existing Circuit City Group will include the Circuit City Superstore business as well as its retained interest in the CarMax Group. The plan includes a public offering of CarMax Group stock that will represent 20% of its equity value.

Circuit City Stores, Inc. is the nation's largest retailer of brand-name consumer electronics and major appliances and a leading retailer of personal computers and music software. Headquartered in Richmond, Virginia, it operates 409 Superstores, five consumer electronics-only stores, and 43 mall-based Circuit City Express Stores.

CarMax is the automotive retail concept developed by Circuit City Stores, Inc. CarMax operates five locations, including single locations in Richmond, Virginia, and Raleigh and Charlotte, North Carolina, and two locations in Atlanta, Georgia. The concept is betting that consumers turned off by the process of buying a used car will prefer to visit national, brand-name superstores like CarMax. The stores offer a large selection, no haggling over price, and the option of returning the car if the customer is not satisfied. CarMax pioneered the idea of selling many auto brands in a friendly, no-hassle environment three years ago, but hasn't made any money. CarMax plans to open 80 to 90 dealerships over the next five years, up from the five it currently operates. CarMax will benefit from Circuit City's favorable access to financing as well as Circuit City's resources and expertise in areas such as consumer credit, media buying, real estate acquisition, and development and management information systems.

The company believes the tracking stock structure will enable it to maximize shareholder value by creating a separately traded stock that reflects the results of the CarMax Group. The company feels the structure should encourage more in-depth coverage and enable investors to better understand and value the business. Further, the market price established for the CarMax Group stock also will facilitate the valuation of the interest that the Circuit City Group will continue to hold, and therefore management believes that this transaction will be a net positive for shareholders.

UNIQUE ISSUES RAISED BY A SPIN-OFF

Allocation Issues

Which businesses and which assets and liabilities will move to the new company? Which company will get the office facilities and equipment that is currently shared? How will contingent liabilities (i.e., taxes, litigation, and environmental), which may relate to both companies, be allocated?

Capital Structure Issues

Will the parent corporation have to seek waivers under its credit facility? What impact will the spin-off have on the company's debt? What structure will the new company need (will it require a new credit facility, or public or private debt)?

Management Issues

Who will run the new company? Who will have employment agreements? Which employees will go to the new company? Will the company have equity-based incentive compensation? How will the pension plan be treated (will a proportionate amount of assets and liabilities be transferred to a pension plan the new company)? Will the restructuring require layoffs?

Accounting Issues

Are any accounting changes necessary for the spin-off? Management should conduct a extensive review of the company's accounting policies to see if they are still valid as a separate entity.

Separation Issues

What will be the continuing relationship between the parent corporation and the new company? Will transition services be provided by the parent to the spin-off for an interim period? Is there a need for ongoing agreements to supply goods or services?

Compliance and Approval Issues

What regulatory approval is necessary or desirable for the spin-off ? Is a shareholder vote needed? Must the securities issued in the spin-off be registered with the SEC? Will the parent corporation be solvent after the spin-off, so as to avoid fraudulent conveyance concerns? Will the divestiture be tax-free per the IRS?

SUMMARY

Evidence exists that stock of both the parent and the spin-off outperform the overall market. A corporate spin-off often boosts the shares of the company shedding the business, as well as the shares of the spin-off.

According to a study by professors James Miles and Randall Woolridge of the Smeal School of Business at Penn State University, spun-off shares tend to outperform their peers and the overall market. The professors looked at 174 spin-offs between 1965 and 1994 and found that, in the first three years the companies were on their own, their prices rose an average 76%. That easily outpaced the S&P 500 stock index's gain by 31 percentage points during the same period.

The following summary was extracted from a study called "Some New Evidence That Spin-Offs Create Value."[2]

The study, by professors James Miles and Randall Woolridge of Penn State University, and Patrick Cusatis of Lehman Brothers, outlines some of the reasons as to why spin-offs tend to do well.

At least two thirds of those spinoffs subsequently acquired were operating in businesses unrelated to their parents and were acquired by firms in related businesses. This is strong evidence that spinoffs help facilitate asset transfers designed to improve corporate focus.

Previous research documents significant shareholder gains from corporate spinoffs. Such work focuses primarily on changes in parent firm share prices at the time of spinoff announcements. The positive abnormal announcement-date stock returns reported for the parent firms presumably reflect investors' expectations of operating improvements by spinoffs and their parents.

Our recent research on 161 tax-free spinoffs over the period of 1965–1990 both confirms and extends this body of work by producing the following findings:

- Parent firms exhibit substandard operating performance prior to spinoffs, but after their spinoffs their performance improves to about average levels.

- As newly independent and separately trading businesses, spinoffs experience significantly faster growth in sales, operating income before depreciation, return on sales, total assets, and capital expenditures than other other comparable firms over the same time period.

- Over the two-year period prior to the spinoff, the stock price of the average parent company outperforms the stock market by 35% on average—a finding we attribute to already ongoing restructuring activities at such companies.

- After the spinoffs, stock returns of both the parent and the spinoff outperform the market, on average.

Continued

- Because both the parent firms and their spinoffs experience a higher rate of takeover activity after the spinoffs than do control groups of similar firms, part of these abnormal returns can be attributed to takeover activity. Nevertheless, even those samples of parents and spinoffs not taken over achieved significant shareholder returns.

- At least two thirds of those spinoffs subsequently acquired were operating in businesses unrelated to their parents' to begin with, and were acquired by firms in related businesses. This is strong evidence that spinoffs help facilitate asset transfers designed to improve corporate focus.

  The question remains as to the reason for the exceptional operating performance by spunoff firms. Our best guess is that spinning off unrelated businesses has two major benefits:

- a more decentralized, market-based capital allocation process, which in turn often leads to increased investment opportunities for spinoffs; and

- a more accountable, focused top management team, often motivated by significant stock holdings.

  Also, in those cases where the spun-off business ends up being acquired by a company in the same line of business, the sequence of transactions leads to better strategic fit.

Patrick Cusatis is a Vice President at Lehman Brothers working in the firm's municipal finance group. James Miles is the Joseph F. Bradley Fellow of Finance at Penn State University. Randall Woolridge is Goldman Sachs & Co. and Frank P. Smeal Fellow of Finance at Penn State University.

Continued

THE INVESTMENT PERFORMANCE OF SPINOFFS

We analyze the investment performance of spinoffs and compare this performance to that of IPOs. Using a sample of 146 pure spinoffs over the 1965–1988 period, we examine portfolio returns for monthly periods up to three years. We evaluate (1) distribution month returns to assess the initial pricing of spinoffs, (2) raw and market adjusted returns for spinoffs presuming monthly portfolio rebalancing for periods up to 36 months, (3) raw and matched-firm adjusted returns for spinoffs presuming both portfolio rebalancing and buy-and-hold investment strategies for periods up to 36 months, and (4) risk-adjusted performance of spinoffs using Ib Botson's (1975) regression across time and securities (RATS) model to estimate abnormal returns. We find that spinoffs perform poorly in their first few months of trading, but over longer periods of time they appear to outperform the market and matched-firms by a significant margin. Over the entire three-year period, assuming portfolio rebalancing, we find a compounded raw return of 106.6%, which corresponds to a compounded annual return of 27.4%. After adjusting for the market using various market return indices, cumulative abnormal performance in the range of 20 to 30 percent is indicated over the three-year period. Likewise, cumulative returns in excess of the returns for firms matched by industry and market capitalization is in excess of 20% over the three-year period. The largest returns come between one and two years after the distribution month. The results are quite similar under both portfolio rebalancing and buy-and-hold investment strategies. Overall, these findings are in direct contrast to results reported for IPOs. Whereas IPOs offer positive abnormal returns at issuance but underperform the market and peers thereafter, spinoffs initially perform poorly but provide positive abnormal returns over an extended period of time. While we do not attempt to identify the determinant(s) of the abnormal stock performance, we speculate that it may be related to (1) superior operating performance generated by a reduction in agency and overhead costs, market as opposed to administrative capital allocation, and/or incentives created by more effective compensation of management, and/or (2) the fact that spinoff allows the subsidiary to attract takeover bids from suitors who place a higher value on its assets.

Spinoff Common Stock Returns
146 Pure Spinoffs over 1965–88 Period

Return   Return

| Raw Returns | — — NASDAQ Adj. | ····· S&P 500 Adj. |
| Sm. Firm Adj. | ·········· Mat. Firm Adj. | |

0   6   12   18   24   30   36

Months Relative to First Trade
*Cumulative Compounded Returns, Assuming Monthly Rebalancing

From Patrick Cusatis, James Miles, and Randall Woolridge, "Some New Evidence That Spin-Offs
Create Value," *Journal of Applied Corporate Finance*, Vol. 7, No. 2, Summer, 1994. Reprinted
with permission.
Reprinted with permission, Department of Finance, College of Business Administration, The
Pennsylvania State University.

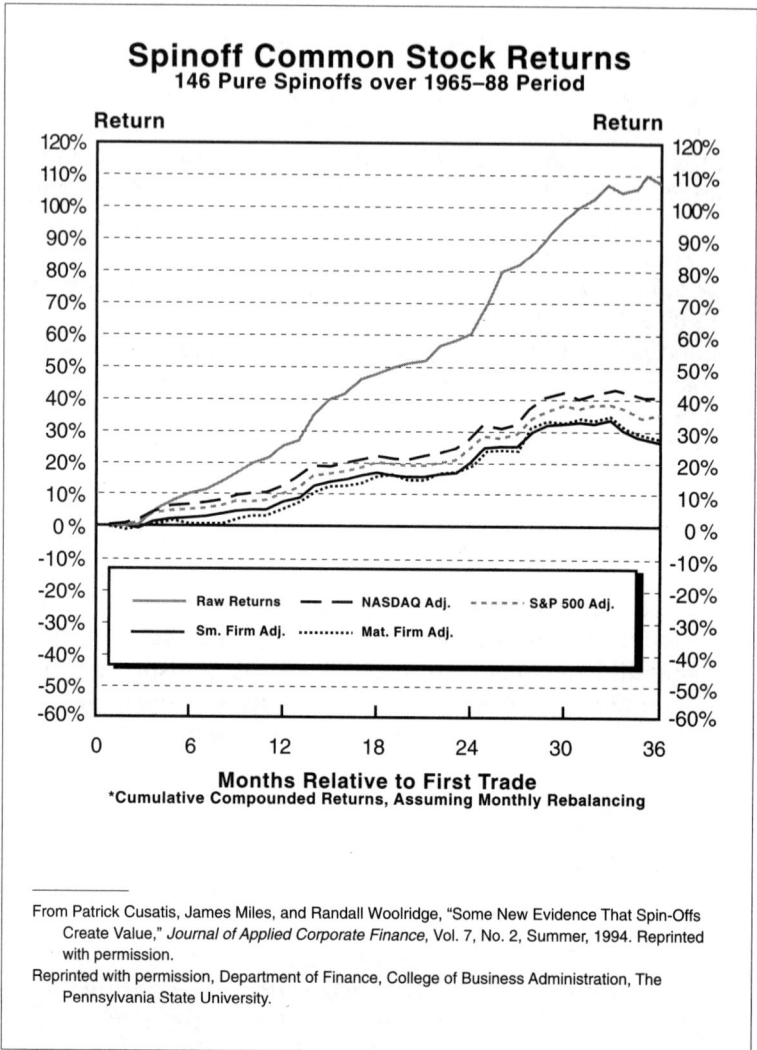

A J.P. Morgan study of 77 spin-offs from 1985 through 1995 shows that spin-offs outperform the stock market by more that 20% on average during the first 18 months after the transaction. The same study found that parent companies outperform the overall stock market by 5 to 6%, on average, between the spin-off announcement date and the actual spin-off.

There is considerable academic research on spin-offs that suggests that they outperform the general market by considerable margin. Hite and Owers, Shipper and Smith, and Miles and Rosenfeld document a mean abnormal spin-off announcement return of approximately 3%.[3]

CHAPTER **2**

Why Spin-Offs Occur

HIGH-QUALITY SPIN-OFFS

It is useful to look at spin-offs as falling (simplistically) into two categories- High or poor quality. This is use to refer to the perceived quality of the stock as an investment at the time of spin-off as opposed to the company itself.

The better quality spin-off is typically a more desirable company whose business may be dissimilar from the parent's core business. Management's hope might be that as a separately traded, more easily analyzed entity, the good subsidiary's earnings would receive a high market valuation. The spin-off of such a business could thus enhance the total value of the parent shareholder's holdings, since it might be valued at little or nothing as part of the current corporate whole. In spinning off a more desirable unit, management may see a stock market opportunity where pure plays in specific sectors are highly prized by investors. In this instance, the spin-off could possibly finance its growth more inexpensively with easier access to low-cost capital.

LOW-QUALITY SPIN-OFFS: THE CORPORATE ORPHANS

Spin-offs that are viewed as lower quality occur more frequently than do high-quality spin-offs. Ironically, the spin-off dogs may present greater investment opportunities than do the best quality spin-offs. The castaways often face significant problems and as a result are frequently unprofitable. While the long-term fundamental outlook for the spin-off's business may be promising, it is often too far off to justify retaining the business in the corporate fold. Parent company management may have lost its patience or ability to deal with the unit's problems. Some of those problems could include significant lawsuits, environmental issues, mature or declining markets, over-large fixed cost structures, and a general history of poor management or even mismanagement.

The benefits of separating problem operations from the parent's relatively untroubled businesses are self evident. For the parent company, perhaps the principal benefit of spinning off a troubled operation is that the market value of the presumably profitable remaining businesses may be enhanced by the elimination of the underperforming assets. Reducing analytical distractions are other benefits of such a spin-off.

COMMONLY ACCEPTED BUSINESS PURPOSES FOR A SPIN-OFF

Equity Financing

One business reason cited for spinning off a portion of a business is because the company believes that a spin-off will allow the parent or a subsidiary to trade at a higher valuation than the current stock price. Again, the IRS is unlikely to accept that simply increasing the stock price enhances the business per se, unless a stock offering to raise capital to be used in the business will follow. Consequently, the IRS will request a letter from an investment banker stating the case for the spin-off as a technique of effecting a more successful stock offering. The IRS will demand a representation that an offering will take place within a year after the spin-off.

Regulatory Relief

An example of a business purpose based on regulatory rules is a divestiture required by a governmental agency. The spin-off may follow an acquisition whose approval by the Federal

Trade Commission or Department of Justice may be contingent on divestiture of a certain businesses.

It can be difficult to document regulatory relief to the satisfaction of the IRS. Many times, a government agency will not mandate that a spin-off take place. Usually, private consul has advised the acquiring company that a spin-off could help avoid certain regulatory restraints. If the divestiture has not been mandated by regulators, a legal opinion may be required to convince the IRS that the spin-off will lead to the desired outcome.

Debt Financing

This business purpose promotes the belief that the company's ability to borrow will be enhanced as a result of the separation of the parent and the subsidiary. The focus would likely be on circumstances affecting the company's credit rating.

Fit and Focus

This purpose often involves a noncore business identified by management. Many spin-offs have received IRS approval based on the parent's ability to show that the needs of one business for management direction and access to capital markets would be greatly improved through separation from one or more other businesses.

Spin-offs make sense for a company in the following situations:

- If the businesses do not share a technology base and have distinctly different research and development approaches. (A spin-off does not make sense if it destroys a common R&D process.)
- If the businesses have different marketing or distribution approaches. (Usually a spin-off does not make sense if the products go through the same channels or use the same marketing strategies.)
- If the businesses require different debt-to-equity ratios to compete in their industries. (For example, ITT Corp.'s restructuring was in part motivated by

the need for its industrial businesses to take on more debt. ITT couldn't increase debt levels without harming the high credit rating needed by ITT Hartford Insurance.)

■ If the spin-off will provide investors with a clearer view of how to value the individual businesses.

CHAPTER 3

Why Invest in Spin-Offs?

The first and foremost reason to invest in spin-offs is, of course, to make money. Numerous academic studies suggest that many spin-offs have experienced significant capital appreciation, both on an absolute and a relative basis. Spin-off pricing inefficiency, where it can be accurately identified, holds the potential for above-average investment returns over time. Nevertheless, factors such as the timing of the initial purchase, length of holding period, and selectivity are critical to successful spin-off investing.

Furthermore, spin-offs are an investment anomaly; as a class of securities, they are often not efficiently priced. Once removed from the corporation, these newly independent spin-offs frequently undergo significant internal and external changes, which can create major investment opportunities and problems in spin-off analysis and investment.

Why are spin-offs priced inefficiently?

1. *Ownership changes rapidly.* As previously discussed, there are a number of "structural" selling effects that help explain why the shares may be misvalued (index fund selling, no yield, odd-lot selling, limited liquidity, etc.). In addition, remember that people are receiving shares that they have not chosen to buy and often have no interest in keeping. This exacerbates the selling pressure.

2. *Inadequate or partial information.* As a group of new securities, spin-offs tend to be less well known. Often, these companies have been hidden inside the corporate fold of the parent for their entire existence. As a subsidiary of a larger company, only partial and incomplete operating and financial information has been available. Because of this, investment advisors often are inclined to suggest selling the spin-off.

For a variety of reasons, there is often an absence of adequate financial information on spin-offs. Management is typically reluctant to provide sufficient information to perform financial analysis procedures due to uncertainties over spin-off effects on earnings. This inevitably leads to valuation difficulties. Therefore, less research is done until more adequate information is available. This naturally leads to the spin-off being underfollowed by Wall Street analysts. This contrasts strongly with an IPO, where roadshows are presented to promote the offering. Also, there is no post-IPO syndicate to support the spin-off stock price in the aftermarket.

3. *Uncertain earnings outlook.* Since many spin-offs are made up of underperforming assets to begin with, it is difficult to target appropriate valuation parameters. It is also difficult to precisely project new expenses the spin-off will incur as a freestanding company, which adds to the difficulty of forecasting earnings and appropriate valuations. In addition, the lack of comparable public companies to provide acceptable valuation comparisons compounds these problems.

4. *Little or no "street research coverage."* The lack of street coverage initially for spin-offs can create excellent opportunities for investors. There is little economic motivation for large brokerage firms to initiate coverage of spun-off companies. Remember that the shares are given to shareholders; therefore, Wall Street cannot make any fees on the distribution. In addition, the typical spin-off is small- to mid-cap in size, further inhibiting Wall Street's interest. Further, management (in the new spin-off) may be ill equipped to deal with investor relations at a sophisticated level. Often, the staff is without adequate, experienced personnel to convey the company's message to investors.

CORPORATE SPIN-OFFS

One of the preeminent trends in the corporate world is the move toward breaking up multibusiness companies and "spinning-off" their components, under the belief that that their size and diversity inhibits competitiveness. Corporate spin-offs have been gathering momentum, fueled by investor pressure to unlock hidden value. In recent years, the use of spin-offs as a means of divestiture has grown dramatically. In 1994, spin-offs represented 26% of all corporate divestitures, up from 10% in 1988.

In a bid to improve shareholder value, many diversified companies are electing to spin-off parts of their business. 1995 saw a record 82 corporate spin-offs nationwide, worth a total of $48 billion. That was nearly twice the 1994 total of 48 spin-offs worth $27 billion, according to Securities Data Corp. 1996 was another record for spin-offs (95 total), as companies continue to discover that this form of divestiture often leads to significantly greater shareholder value.

In an age where agility and flexibility are necessary for corporate survival, more and more companies are splitting into distinct components. This pronounced trend will continue as companies focus on their core competencies rather than attempting to diversify operating results. Wall Street tends to assign higher P/E ratios to firms focused on one industry, so splitting a company can result in a higher overall valuation.

Tax Advantages

The spin-off has become a popular way of increasing the value of a corporation while taking advantage of tax laws. The spin-off distribution can be made tax-free to the parent corporation and the receiving shareholder. This can represent significant savings to the parent company, relative to selling the division outright, if the subsidiary is carried on the books at a large discount to current market value. A sale would generate a sizable capital gain tax. However, if at least 80% of a

FIGURE 3-1

Spin-Off Volume
Number of Deals

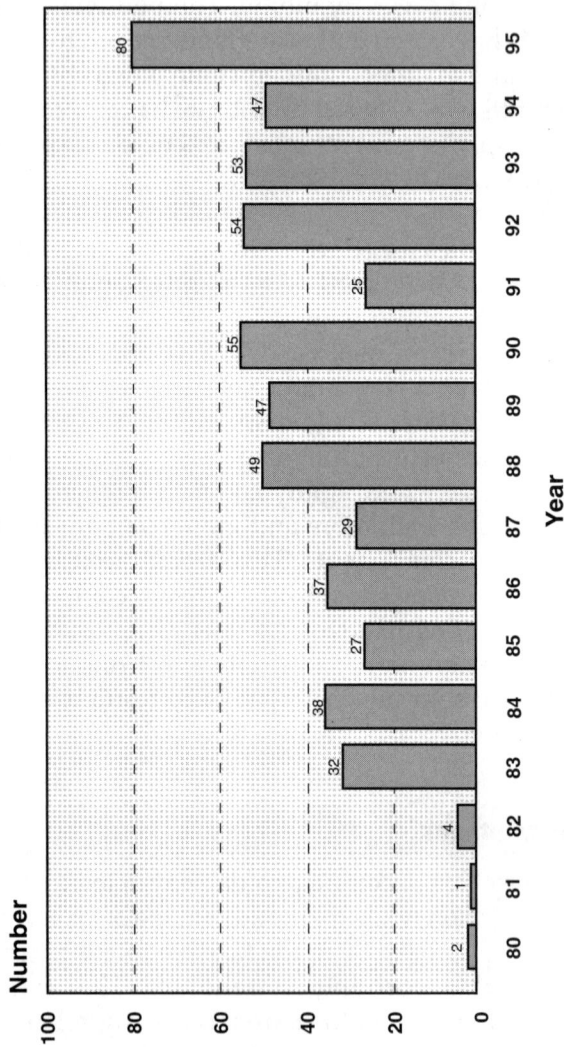

Source: Securities Data Company.

FIGURE 3-2

Spin-Off Volume
Dollar Amount

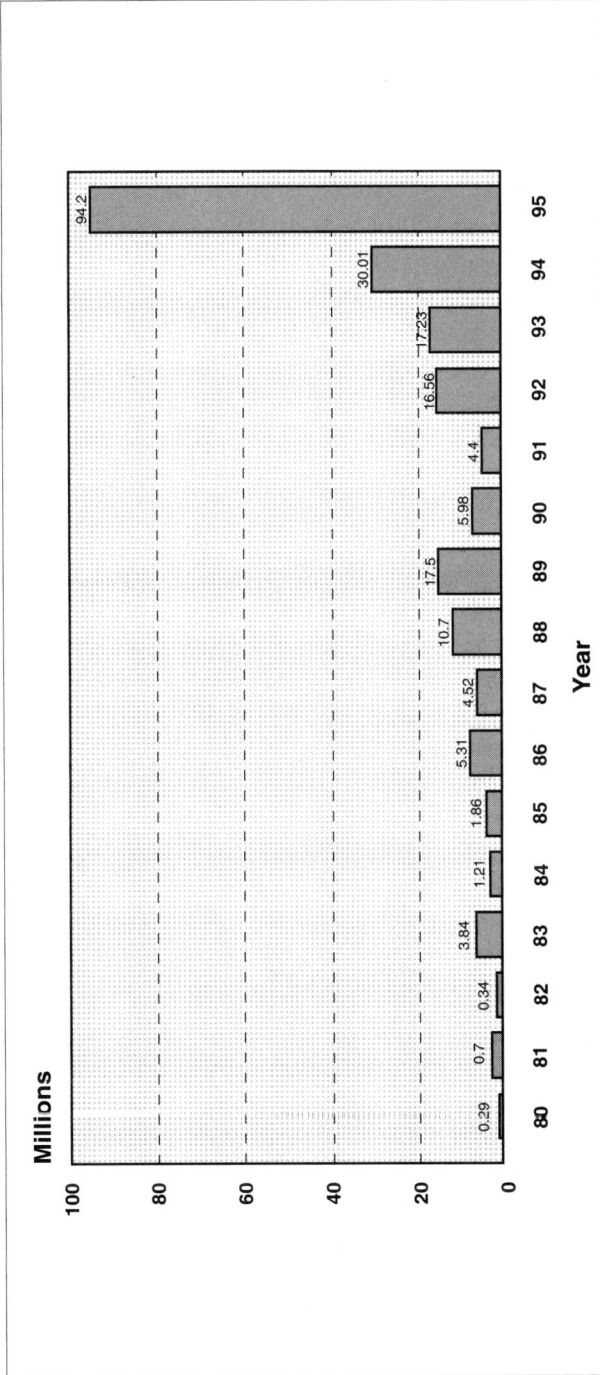

Millions

Year	Amount
80	0.29
81	0.7
82	0.34
83	3.84
84	1.21
85	1.86
86	5.31
87	4.52
88	10.7
89	17.5
90	5.98
91	4.4
92	16.56
93	17.23
94	30.01
95	94.2

Source: Securities Data Company.

subsidiary's equity is distributed to existing shareholders, a company can avoid that capital gains tax liability.

Spin-offs are the most tax-efficient mechanism for separating a division. The parent firm restructures the subsidiary as an independent company with its own stock, then gives those shares to current investors of the parent company. Under Internal Revenue Service rules, to qualify for a spin-off, the dividend company must have been in business for at least five years to obtain tax-free status. The Securities and Exchange Commission also requires three years of audited financials.

Spin-offs are one of three basic ways to divest a subsidiary. The other two methods are sell-offs (usually for cash, where the subsidiary is sold to another corporation or to the division's management in a leveraged buyout [LBO]) and equity carve-outs, also known as partial public offerings, in which some or all of the subsidiary's stock is offered directly to the public in the form of an IPO.

From a shareholder standpoint, the spin-off, based on distribution of stock in a subsidiary to create a new public company, is the most attractive restructuring alternative. Why? Spin-offs differ from the other two methods in several ways, but the most significant is that spin-offs that qualify under Internal Revenue Service Code Section 355 are the only way to divest assets on a tax-free basis. The tax-efficiency of a pure spin-off is a major reason corporations have increasingly opted to divest divisions in this manner.

Requirements for a Tax-Free Spin-Off

In order to effectively execute a spin-off, complex rules must be followed to ensure that the unit will be able to operate independently, that the transaction is tax-free, and the financial reporting requirements are satisfied. Particular care must be paid to capital structure, IRS rules, and financial reporting requirements. Significant preparation is necessary to execute a spin-off so that the division is ready to operate on its own. Critical issues to contemplate include the establishment of the division's business purpose, creation of a capital structure, and allocation of costs and debt.

For a distribution to be tax-exempt it must meet the criteria set forth in Internal Revenue Code Section 355. If a spin-off fails to meet all of the section's requirements, the company will be liable for the full taxes on the divestiture without receiving the cash that could be used to pay the tax bill. In addition, shareholders will be taxed on the receipt of an ordinary income dividend. In order to be tax-free, among other things, the spin-off must be undertaken for a bona fide, nontax, "corporate business purpose" (to save costs, other than federal taxes; to enhance the profitability of the new company; and to enhance management focus on each business). The parent must "control" the subsidiary to be spun off immediately prior to the spin-off, and the parent must distribute "control" of the subsidiary to the parent's shareholders. The shareholders of the parent corporation must maintain a "continuity of interest" in both the parent corporation and the spun-off subsidiary.

Finally, the parent corporation and the spun-off subsidiary must actively conduct a trade or business immediately after the spin-off, and the business must have been actively conducted throughout the five-year period ending on the date of the spin-off.

To avoid taxable consequences, the transaction must be structured carefully to abide to the rules of Code Section 355, which are summarized as follows:

Control: The parent company must have "control" of the subsidiary immediately prior to the spin-off and must disburse to the shareholders a controlling amount of subsidiary stock. Normally, the parent is required to distribute all of its stock in the subsidiary. Control is defined as stock possessing at least 80% of the voting power and at least 80% of each class of nonvoting stock.

Active business: Code Section 355 also requires that both the parent and subsidiary be engaged immediately after the spin-off in an active trade or business in which each has actively operated for at least five years prior to the divestiture.

May not be used as a device to avoid taxation: Under the
code, the transaction must not be used as a device to
distribute earnings of a company. Basically, this means
that the transaction may not be used simply as a
means of escaping dividend taxation rules by convert-
ing ordinary income into capital gains.

Transaction must have a substantial business purpose: The
most rigorous requirement for a tax-free spin-off is
that the transaction have a substantial business purpose. This is typically the most rigorous and uncertain
prerequisite. Through the years, a business test has
evolved through Internal Revenue Service rulings and
court cases. This test requires that the spun-off company have a real and substantial business purpose
separate from avoiding federal income taxes. Commonly, a spin-off must bring about material and
quantifiable cost savings or other benefits to one or
more of the businesses involved.

Ironically, enhancing shareholder value is not an
acceptable business purpose to the IRS. Clearly, the
IRS understands that increasing shareholder value is
the driving force guiding many CEOs' decisions to
restructure via spin-offs. Nevertheless, the IRS remains adamant about the necessity to demonstrate
some immediate good for the business itself.

Continuity of interest: This rule requires that the shareholders of the parent maintain a significant, continuing interest in both the parent and the subsidiary
following the transaction.

WHY SPIN-OFFS PROSPER

Much of the spin-off's impressive performance comes from
the altered dynamics of the spun-off business and its parent.
Spin-offs tend to do well partly because newly independent
managers have greater freedom of action to pursue new ventures, streamline production methods, and pare overhead.
In addition, they have better access to expansion capital. As
a subsidiary, the company likely had to beg for capital to grow

the business. Newly independent managers are offered stock options and compensation packages tied to performance of the independent unit. This often imbues them with entrepreneurial zeal. As a result, performance revs up. According to the Penn State study, the operating income of spin-off companies and their parents improves significantly after separation.

Many spin-offs also post market-beating results because they are five times more likely than similar stand-alone companies to be acquired, often within several years of their distribution. In addition, it is easier for the market to place a rational valuation on each individual operation. Wall Street generally applies a premium on "pure plays." The market values of the sum of a firm's parts proves to be greater that the whole.

CONGLOMERATES—THE END OF AN ERA

The word "conglomerate" came into vogue during the 1960s as a term for a hodgepodge of different units operating under the same parent. It's derived from the Latin verb, *conglomerare*, to roll together into a ball. On Wall Street, a conglomeration was the preeminent innovation in the corporate world—a company that operated in disparate and unrelated businesses.

Conventional wisdom on Wall Street in the 1960s embraced conglomerates, rewarding them with premium price/earnings multiples. Some of the high-flying conglomerates in the past were ITT (which recently spun-off into three publicly traded companies), Litton Industries, Gulf & Western, and General Electric. These were the glamour stocks of the late 1950s because they grew rapidly by trading their high P/E stock for the cheaper shares of other companies in mundane businesses.

The aim of conglomerates was to smooth out the earnings volatility inherent in the business cycle. Companies bought unrelated businesses in order to diversify sales and earnings. Wall Street hailed the conglomerates as the embodiment of a new business philosophy, the idea that a CEO was not really in the business of making a product, but rather of maximizing the return on his capital and thereby raising the value of his company's stock.

Unfortunately, conglomerates have proven to be a poor idea. Excessive diversification tends to separate management talents and interest from the running of a particular business. It is very difficult for top management to make decisions without a deep, hands-on knowledge for the business. Managers running operating divisions of conglomerates tend to feel neglected and abused by the bureaucrats at headquarters, who oversee budgets and allocate capital but know little about the particular business.

Conglomerates are usually accorded a discount in their stock valuation by investors because they are difficult to understand and analyze. Investors do not need invest in a conglomerate to diversify. With many thousands of mutual funds available these days, investors can easily create their own diversified portfolio. Thus, it is not necessary to own a company with many diverse businesses in order to garner the benefits of diversification. This has ushered in the era of the spin-off. It seems likely this form of disaggregation (the breakup of larger, less synergistic businesses into separate entities), which is taking place at unprecedented levels, will continue.

Businesses can be disposed of in many ways, including a sale to another company, a leveraged buyout by the managers of the company, or an initial public offering. However, to reiterate, the spin-off is the most tax-efficient.

CHAPTER 4

Spin-Offs
Are Misvalued

Spin-offs, somewhat paradoxically, are brand-new companies that have in many cases existed for years. Suddenly thrown out of the corporate fold, these newly independent companies frequently undergo significant internal and external changes, which can create major investment opportunities.

The mechanics of a spin-off vary. In a pure spin-off, a company splits off a business unit, either a division or subsidiary, and distributes that part to shareholders on a tax-free basis. Each shareholder receives a pro-rated distribution of the entire spun-off unit. The shareholder ends up with stock in two separate companies—a slimmed down parent and a newly independent spin-off. This process stands in sharp contrast to an initial public offering (IPO), in which the parent company is actually selling (rather than giving away) some or all of its ownership interest in a subsidiary. As a result, spin-offs are in effect new issues, but there is no underwriter or promoter telling the investment community what the company is worth.

One observation can be made from analyzing how the spin-off company's stock underperforms the S&P 500 during the initial few months as a separately traded company.[1] This phenomenon suggests that the average stock experienced significant selling pressure during that period. To a large degree, the selling pressure can be attributable to the actions

53

of institutional investors. Many portfolio managers are forced to stay within predetermined investment guidelines that decrease risk and liability arising from issues related to fiduciary responsibility. Typical investment criteria include the following factors: firm size (i.e., is the firm included in the S&P 500?); volatility; dividend yield; liquidity; market capitalization; minimum quality standards; and leverage. A corporate spin-off that does not meet threshold standards may be deemed an inappropriate investment and sold. Often spin-offs trade below where they should in relation to their intrinsic values. Spin-offs as a class of security can often be excellent for ferreting out value. Ownership changes occur rapidly. Companies frequently have inadequate or partial information (both on a historical and a projected basis) and an uncertain earnings outlook. Formal "street" research analysis is typically minimal initially, because there is little economic incentive for Wall Street to follow these obscure often smaller companies.

In addition, there is initially selling pressure from index funds that is structural in nature. For example, perhaps the parent company is in the S&P 500 index; however, the subsidiary that is being spun-off will not be part included in the index. Index funds are designed to mimic an index; therefore they are forced to sell the spun-off shares if they are going to continue to mirror the results of the index. This structural selling by index funds puts downward pressure on the spin-off's stock price.

Individual investors who own shares in the parent prior to the divestiture also contribute to the selling pressure on the spin-off. For example, perhaps they owned 200 shares in the parent company and, shortly after the spin-off, received 50 shares in the newly spun-off company. They will often sell these shares for a variety of reasons. Some think of the spin-off stock as found money and cash out immediately. Others do not wish to deal in odd lots and sell. Individuals may not find the business or industry promising enough to warrant holding. Investment brokers can perhaps generate two trades if they can prod the investor into selling the spun-off company and buying something the firm covers. This contributes to the initial weakness typically seen in a newly spun-off firm.

These factors, coupled with the lack of sufficient trading volume in the unseasoned spin-off, can create significant
downward pressure during the first few months of trading.
Selling pressure on the stock provides the astute investor opportunities to purchase spin-offs at favorable prices. In this
book I will present some of the investment lessons that I have
observed from reviewing the price-performance history of
recent spin-offs. Many spin-offs offer the potential for above-
average investment returns. Some spin-offs have shown dramatic price appreciation since being spun-off. Nevertheless,
factors such as timing of initial purchase, length of holding
period, and selectivity are as critical to successful spin-off
investing as they would be for almost any category of investment.

Empirical research shows that stock values increase as
a result of spin-offs. Indeed, spin-offs appear to offer a "free-
lunch" in what is otherwise considered a relatively efficient
equity market. This would contradict the efficient market
hypothesis (EMH), which argues that the stock market is efficient and stock prices reflect all existing information. However, ever since Rolf Banz uncovered the small-firm effect
(small stocks outperform big stocks), academics have ques-
tioned the degree of stock market efficiency and exposed the
existence of a number of investment anomalies that challenge
the efficient market hypothesis.

The evidence from a large body of research suggests
what Wall Street practitioners have known intuitively: Pockets of inefficiency exist and hold promise for the astute investor. In the past two decades, academics have uncovered
various anomalies like the small-firm effect, such as the January effect, the low P/E ratio effect, and the low price-to-book
ratio effect.

I suggest that spin-offs too, are inefficient and offer the
astute investor an excellent opportunity for excess investment
returns. Spin-offs often result in a higher aggregate value for
the constituent pieces. This is the inescapable conclusion I
drew from my review of selected corporate spin-offs that
occurred during the last 20 years.

STRUCTURAL SELLING EFFECTS

As previously touched on, there are a number of structural or organic reasons that spin-offs trade lower after being separated from their parent.. For example, if the parent company is included in a major stock index and the spin-off is not, index-fund-selling usually generates selling pressure on the divested company. A large spin-off ratio (1 for 10 or greater, for example) will intensify selling pressure as investors who are not interested in keeping small or odd-lot positions in an unfamiliar company offer those shares. Lack of a dividend may push income-oriented investors out of the spun-off stock. A spin-off of a small-capitalization stock from a large-capitalization stock may prompt large-cap managers to sell due to liquidity concerns.

Spin-offs are often hidden inside the folds of the corporate parent for their entire existence. As a result, only partial and incomplete operating and financial information may be accessible. Taking these conditions into account, brokers and financial advisors are often prone to recommend the sale of spin-offs. In fact, if the broker can persuade his client to sell the untested spin-off and buy a security that he or the firm follows, he can generate two commissions. This selling activity by retail investors contributes to the stock price declines associated with fresh spin-offs.

Many institutional portfolio managers are forced to realign their portfolios to meet preset investment criteria. In other words, if the spin-off does not fall within the manager's investment parameters (size, yield, industry, etc.), it may be necessary to sell the shares without regard to the prospects for a spin-off. This typical structural selling often pushes spin-offs to price levels that are not reflective of the long-term outlook for the company. Savvy investors can take advantage of this temporary decline in prices by accumulating shares on the cheap.

There are no hard and fast rules regarding how long this window of opportunity may exist. It could be as little as a few weeks to more than a year, depending on several factors. But spin-offs with promising longer-term fundamentals should be purchased no later than six months after the spin-off. Price performance suggests that this is typically an optimal period to selectively buy this class of securities. Buying at this time would have yielded the maximum price appreciation over the ensuing 12 to 24 months.

Valuation Difficulties

As explained, initially there is often an absence of adequate financial information about spin-offs. Management can be reluctant to provide sufficient information to perform basic financial analysis due to internal uncertainties over spin-off effects on earnings. The lack of information dissemination leads to valuation difficulties, and consequently less research is done until more information is available. Spin-offs tend to be underfollowed by Wall Street analysts, which helps explain some of the pricing inefficiency.

New Spin-Offs Lack Investor Relations

The new management of a spin-off is often not equipped to deal with investor relations in a sophisticated manner. The new corporate staff typically has no experience in communicating with analysts, money managers, and other Wall Street participants and may find itself without the proper personnel to carry the company's message to investors. Too often, an individual is thrust into the role of communicating with investors without any prior experience in that role. This is especially true with the smaller capitalization spin-offs.

5

Evaluating Spin-Offs

EXAMINE SPIN-OFFS ON A STOCK-BY-STOCK BASIS

Each spin-off is exposed to a wide range of unique pressures that vary in number and severity from stock to stock. Some of the questions that need to be answered about each spin-off are:

Is the spin-off or parent part of a major index?

How similar or disparate is the spin-off's business in relation to the parent?

Is the parent widely sponsored by Wall Street?

How many analysts follow the corporate parent?

Does it pay a dividend?

Where is the stock listed?

All of these issues need to be considered in order to discern if and when to invest in a spin-off. Spin-off performance in recent years suggests that the optimal period to selectively buy this category of stocks is no later that six months after the spin-off.

To further evaluate the investment potential of a particular spin-off stock, the following key questions need to be fully considered by the investor.

Is the Spin-Off Included in a Major Equity Index?

If the corporate parent is included in a major market index and the spin-off is not, sooner or later the index funds will tend to be sellers of the stock. This will tend to depress the spin-off initially.

Does it Pay a Dividend?

If a dividend-paying corporate parent spins off a non-dividend payer, the spin-off will experience selling pressure. Both individuals and institutions can have income needs or requirements that would lead to the sale of a spin-off that does not pay dividends.

Is the Spin-Off's Business Dissimilar to the Parent's?

When the business of the spin-off is dissimilar to that of the corporate parent, there is a greater possibility of an initial investment opportunity. This can be compounded when the spin-off is perceived to have significant operating problems. When the business of the spin-off is similar to that of the parent, there will tend to be fewer investment opportunities because the group of analysts following the parent company are already familiar with the spin-off's business. Thus, opinions will be more uniform as to where the stock should be trading.

What Is the Distribution Ratio?

Spin-offs with high distribution ratios (for example, one spin-off share for each 20 or more corporate parent shares) can create selling pressure as investors eliminate their odd lot holdings.

Is the Spin-Off Taxable?

Taxable spin-offs could experience more selling pressure than tax-free ones. This may occur as some investors sell their shares in order to pay taxes on the spin-off distribution.

RULES OF THUMB

There are a number of factors that can influence price performance of spin-offs.

1. *If the business of the spin-off is similar to the parent, there will tend to be fewer initial investment opportunities.* This is possibly because analysts following the parent company are familiar with the spin-off's business. Thus, initially, one would expect consensus opinions will be more uniform as to where the stock should be trading.

2. *When the business of the spin-off is dissimilar to that of the corporate parent, there is a greater possibility of an initial investment opportunity.* This can be particularly true when the spin-off is perceived to have significant operating problems.

3. *If the parent pays a dividend and the spin-off is non-dividend paying, the spin-off will likely experience selling pressure.* Individuals and institutions that have income needs or must adhere to yield requirements would be expected to sell the non-dividend paying spin-off. For example, some little bank in Iowa managing a trust portfolio would rather not fool around with a unfamiliar security with questionable prospects. The bank would sell the stock immediately.

4. *If the parent is in an index and the spin-off is not, sooner or later the index fund will have to sell off the shares.* This can lead to considerable selling in light of the large amount of money that is indexed in order to mimic a particular market.

5. *Spin-offs with high distribution ratios (i.e., 1 spin-off share for 10 of parent) create selling as investors eliminate odd-lot positions.* Some investors do not care to have small or fractional positions and are inclined to view the spin-off as "found money" and sell shortly after the distribution.

SPIN-OFF CAVEATS

- The favorable returns have happened during a very strong market backdrop—in an extended bull market. When the business cycle turns down it will likely be especially hard on new spin-offs cut from their parents' deep pockets.

- Spin-offs are not always the tonic for an overburdened parent or a guaranteed boost for neglected subsidiaries.
- There are no universal axioms for evaluating corporate spin-offs. What is right for one company may not be right for another. Spin-offs require as much security analysis as any other equity investment. You have to be a stock picker. The spin-off must still be a fundamentally good business.
- Often a parent seems less concerned with increasing shareholder value than with improving its own balance sheet. Some spin-off subsidiaries begin life on their own with substantial debt weighting them down. If the business cycle is accommodating, it may not be a problem, but when business conditions take a turn for the worse the spun-off company will not have a deep-pocketed parent to bail it out.

CONFLICT BETWEEN BONDHOLDERS AND SHAREHOLDERS

Other considerations for spin-off evaluation concern the debt versus equity interests of the respective shareholders.

Even if shareholders have reason to be pleased with spin-offs, bondholders may protest. Why? Some debt may be less creditworthy after a spin-off. If a company with significant assets and cash flows is spun off, bondholders can be left with less money to satisfy their claims. (Some have suggested that the excess returns afforded to equity holders of spin-offs result in part because bondholders are less well off). Therefore spin-off transactions can raise the legal issue of fraudulent conveyance, wherein assets are sheltered from parties who may have a financial or legal claim on them.

The conflict that can arise between shareholders and bondholders was clearly illustrated by Marriott Corp.'s 1993 spin-off of its hotel management subsidiary, Marriott International. Almost all of the debt was retained by the parent, renamed Host Marriott, which owned the hotel properties.

Shareholders were delighted with the terms of the transaction. Shares in Host Marriott and Marriott International both showed substantial gains after the spin-off. Bondholders were not so pleased. Without the cash flow from Marriott International, their bonds were downgraded by Moody's and dropped by as much as 30% in value.

In summary, the impact of spin-offs on bondholders is at best neutral and generally has negative credit rating implications.

CHAPTER **6**

Timing the Purchase and Sale of the Spin-Off

SELL QUICKLY AFTER THE SPIN-OFF

As previously discussed, spin-offs can very often be purchased at lower stock prices after the initial period of trading. On average there is a negative cumulative return for
spin-off stocks for the first several months of trading. Once
the initial selling pressure abates, spin-offs tend to greatly
outperform the S&P during the following six months to three
years (see study by Pat Cusatis of Lehman Brothers and James
Miles and J. Randall Woolridge of Penn State in Chapter One).
As with all generalizations, there have been many exceptions
to this rule that reinforce the need to inspect each spin-off
independently.

There are many reasons spin-offs face intense selling
pressure during the first few months of trading. If spun-off
from a component of the Standard & Poor's 500 stock index,
these corporate offspring are frequently unloaded by index
funds creating downward pressure on the stock. Also, often
the spun-off company does not pay a dividend, so institutions that require dividend-paying stocks (such as a bank trust
department) will abandon spin-offs, thus adding more selling pressure. Individuals who may not be sophisticated
enough to analyze the prospects of an unknown company
may just view the spin-off as found money and sell. Spin-
offs with high distribution ratios (for example, 1 spin-off share

for each 10 or more corporate parent shares) can create selling pressure as investors eliminate their odd-lot holdings.

Because of this structural selling, spin-offs are often misvalued in the early weeks and months of trading.

> *Spin-offs with promising longer term fundamentals should be re-
> purchased, or initially purchased, no later that six months after the
> spin-off.*

The performance of spin-offs in recent years suggests
this to be the optimal period to selectively buy this these type
of securities. Buying at the post-spin-off lows would have
yielded the maximum price appreciation over the ensuing
12 to 18 months.

WHEN SHOULD YOU INVEST?

There are three periods during which an investor can get involved with a spin-off. Each period presents different investment opportunities and analytical problems. Since many
spin-offs are made up of underperforming assets to begin
with, it is difficult to target appropriate buying or selling
points based on traditional valuation parameters. The difficulty in accurately projecting new expenses the new spin-off
can expect to incur as a freestanding company adds to the
difficulty of forecasting earnings and appropriate valuations.

The Pre-Spin Period

The pre-spin period occurs after a spin-off is announced. The
decision to buy stock in the corporate parent may be desirable if it enables the investor to purchase both entities at a
lower combined price than the two, separate, post-spin-off
companies. But this can be difficult without definitive knowledge of the spin-off's balance sheet, asset base, and normal-
ized earnings power.

Typically, the market reacts positively to spin-off announcements. Often there will be an initial jolt to the price of
the stock, as investors anticipate increased operating efficiencies that are consistent with these transactions. Several studies have examined the market reaction to the announcement

of carve-outs (Schipper and Smith, 1986) and spin-offs (Hite and Owens, 1983; Miles and Rosenfeld, 1983; and Schipper and Smith, 1983). These studies demonstrated that the announcement of a corporate spin-off or carve-out is associated with positive stock price movements in the parent's stock.

This positive announcement effect is attributable to Wall Street participants embracing the idea that a divestiture will be a catalyst in unlocking value inherent in the business. As the initial euphoria subsides, the stock often settles into a narrow trading range until the actual spin-off takes place. This can be as long as a year or more, depending on the firm seeking IRS, SEC, and final board approval. This can be an attractive time to get involved with the spin-off if one is patient and believes both parts are attractive investments.

The Initial Trading Period

The initial trading period occurs when the actual spin-off occurs, and continues for a period of several weeks to several months. Institutional holders normally are not very active in "when-issued" trading, preferring to take physical receipt of their shares. Thus, if you wish to play the percentages (spin-offs often drop initially), or believe the spin-off's prospects are poor near term, this can be a good window to sell shares. As previously discussed, newly spun-off shares are often subjected to a downward selling pressure due to "structural" issues. If the parent is included in a major index and the spin-off is not, index fund selling generates downward pressure on the spin-off. A large spin-off distribution ratio (i.e., 1 for 20) can intensify selling pressure. Some investors are not interested in holding small or fractional positions in a unfamiliar company. A spin-off of a small-capitalization stock from a large-capitalization stock may prompt large-cap managers to bail out on the spin-off. For these reasons and others, a spin-off often faces significant selling pressure when initially freed from its corporate parent. Therefore, those who are adept traders may wish to consider selling as soon as possible, then repurchase the shares as the selling subsides.

The Seasoning Period

The seasoning period starts from the moment the spin-off is announced and can last up to several years. The better the spin-off is understood and perceived, the faster the seasoning period. During this time more information becomes available, management tells its story to Wall Street, and more realistic appraisals of the company's prospects can be made. Depending on how much structural selling the spin-off endured, this period can contain the greatest mispricing of a given stock as well as the best opportunity to profit from that market inefficiency.

Beware of Buying Too Soon

In the good old days (i.e., the 1980s), buying a spin-off in the early weeks of trading, due to the intensity of artificial selling pressures, was generally the best strategy. However, greater patience and selectivity is more important in ferreting out attractive spin-offs nowadays. Spin-offs tend to trade at higher initial prices than in the 80s, and due to the stellar price performance of some earlier spin-offs, more attention is being paid to this class of security. Consequently, there is now a greater initial interest in the spin-off and less likelihood of grossly mispriced issues relative to their inherent value.

Newly spun-off companies are often subjected to a variety of new and unexpected internal and external pressures. These pressures can have a major effect on its ability to meet initial short-term earnings targets and thus match earnings expectations. If disappointments occur, investors can prove less patient with a company that is suddenly viewed as having no long-term operating record and an uncertain future. The lack of a long-established "sponsorship" with the understanding and willingness to take a longer-term point of view can also hurt the stock price.

PART **TWO**

FOR THE RECORD—
A LOOK AT THE PAST
AND FUTURE

CHAPTER 7

Completed Spin-Offs

Parent	Spin-Off	Spin-Off Date
Adolph Coors Co. (ACCOB)	ACX Technologies (ACTX)	12/21/92

ACX Technologies was born when Coors Co., third largest brewer in the United States, spun off nonbeer assets to shareholders. These assets were involved in high-tech ceramics, aluminum, and packaging. Coors decided it was missing good opportunities in its outside businesses. Nor were the values of the nonbeer businesses reflected in Coors' stock price. In December 1992, Coors packaged its nonbeer assets into ACX Technologies and distributed ACX to Coors shareholders on the basis of one share for every three shares of Coors. By separating the nonbeer businesses from the main beer business, the Coors family was in a better position to reward executives on what their businesses did rather than on what the whole company did. The ceramics division has performed particularly well, producing high-tech ceramics, which are very hard, nonconductive, and heat resistant and are used in products such as car ignitions, antilock brakes, and cellular phones.

The packaging division has also done well since being liberated from its parent. ACX owns a patented method for laminating cardboard with a low-cost metallized film, which is almost entirely recyclable. The spin-off highlighted the hidden value, and significant shareholder value was created.

Parent	Spin-Off	Spin-Off Date
Alco Standard Corp. (ASN)	Unisource Worldwide, Inc. (UWW)	1/2/97

Alco Standard distributes paper, packaging products, and office equipment. Prior to the spin-off, Alco Standard conducted two principal businesses: Unisource's businesses and the office solutions business of IKON, formerly referred to as Alco Office products, Inc., which sells and leases copiers, fax machines, and other office equipment to food processors and offers related maintenance services, facilities management, and specialized document-copying services. The company provides one-stop shopping to customers who seek quality, accessible office productivity solutions. Unisource Worldwide distributes office and printing papers to printers and other businesses, paper and plastic packaging and related equipment to food processors, and janitorial supplies to commercial facilities.

One share of Unisource common stock was distributed for every two shares of Alco stock owned as of December 13, 1996. Regular trading in Unisource started on the New York Stock Exchange on January 2, 1997. UWW started trading at around $20 per share. Approximately 66.3 million shares of Unisource common stock was distributed in the spin-off.

Early in 1996, Alco's board announced its plan to separate Alco and Unisource into two publicly traded companies in order to eliminate competitive conflict at the customer level and create pure plays in two companies. The spin-off will allow direct investment in two industry leaders: Alco's IKON Office Solutions, which has the largest network of independent copier and office equipment dealers in North America and the United Kingdom, and Unisource, which is the largest marketer and distributor of printing and imaging and supply systems products and services in North America.

Management believes that, following the spin-off, the financial markets will be able to focus on the individual strengths of Alco and Unisource and evaluate more accurately the performance of each distinct business. Each company will be able to pursue opportunities without internal competitive conflict. In addition, separate Alco and Unisource incentive compensation arrangements for key employees, directly related to the performance of ASN, and UWW's common stock will provide enhanced direct incentives for performance. The divestiture will give each company direct access to capital markets and stock-based acquisition currency to finance expansion and growth opportunities

The spin-off was motivated in large part by the growing strategic conflict between IKON and Unisource at the customer level. To capture opportunities created by the availability of high-volume, high-resolution copiers, IKON expanded its business to offer facilities management services, including copy center, mailroom, and other centralized office services for corporate customers. IKON's centers compete with commercial printers and office superstores, which are Unisource customers. This has compromised business from Unisource's large established paper accounts and has reduced Unisource's ability to gain additional market share in the paper market. The spin-off will enable both companies to maximize their own opportunities and stem the customer defections at Unisource.

Parent	Spin-Off	Spin-Off Date
Allen Group (ALN)	Transpro (TPR)	10/2/95

Allen Group, Inc., manufactures mobile-communications products including mobile and base antennas, cellular phones, pagers, and telecommunications products, primarily for commercial and law-enforcement use. On June 15, 1995, Allen Group announced the spin-off of Transpro Inc. (ratio 1:4). Transpro produces heat-transfer and fabricated-metal products for the heavy-duty truck, industrial, and off-road markets. Also, metal products are fabricated for a variety of industries, including truck conversions for Ford Motor Company and van conversions for commercial fleets. The company's products include four-door pickup-truck cabs, aluminum-charger air coolers, radiators, and radiator and heater cores. The purpose of the spin-off was to allow Allen

Group to focus on the emerging trend in the fast-growing wireless telecom industry, while enabling the mature, cyclical truck products group to be separately capitalized.

Transpro (spun-out of the Allen Group in the fourth quarter of 1995), has been under pressure, due to the loss of a Ford contract that should begin to impact results in calendar year 1998. Transpro derives approximately half of its revenue from the aftermarket and the other from OEM component supply to various markets. The aftermarket tends to be less cyclical and generates a modestly higher internal growth rate than the OEM market. In its current structure, Transpro consists of three operating units: GDI (aftermarket light vehicle radiator business); G&O (OEM commercial vehicle radiator business); and Crown (metal fabrication business).

GDI-Transpro is the number-two supplier of aftermarket radiators in the United States. TPR is the exclusive supplier of radiators to Auto Zone and Pep Boys, two of the fastest growing players in the retail distribution of automotive parts. Transpro's aftermarket radiator business is essentially the assets of a partnership between Allen Heat Transfer Products and Handy & Harman Radiator Company. In 1995, when Transpro was formally spun out of the Allen Group, the company acquired Handy & Harman's interest in the operation and began to account for the operation as a wholly owned subsidiary. The company makes radiator cores, replacement radiators, heaters, and cooling system products.

G&O supplies heat exchange equipment to the OEM commercial vehicle market and accounts for 16% of total company sales. TPR makes a variety of products, including radiator assemblies and components. The largest market for these products is the heavy-duty commercial vehicle market. The three largest customers are Paccar, Mack, and Oshkosh Trucks. The G&O division will be folded in with GDI, the aftermarket radiator business. These operations will share the same administrative staff and some overhead. This should enable Transpro to position its radiator business as a full-service supplier across multiple markets.

Crown accounts for 35% of revenues and is a specialty contract manufacturer, with an emphasis on sheet metal fabrication. The business has two main segments: Ford subassembly and miscellaneous sheet metal fabrication. This division took a major blow when Ford did not renew its contract for the next generation of Ford crew cabs in calendar year 1998. Crown currently assembles full crew cab assemblies for Ford pick-up trucks from sheet metal supplied by outside vendors.

Transpro is a good example of a spin-off that is underfollowed and unloved. The stock should benefit from increased exposure as the company develops a track record as a public company and restructuring benefits take hold. Transpro appears cheap based on cash flow, book, and sales multiples. Clearly, the loss of the Ford business is depressing the valuation of TPR's stock price.

Parent	Spin-Off	Spin-Off Date
American Express (AXP)	Lehman Brothers (LEH)	5/31/94

American Express completed the spin-off of Lehman Brothers through a tax-free dividend to shareholders. Regular way trading commenced May 31, 1994. Shareholders received one share of Lehman Brothers for every five shares of American Express owned. The divestiture enabled American Express to focus on its core business of charge cards, banking, and financial services. Lehman Brothers is an investment banking firm. The company's businesses include underwriting, corporate finance, merchant banking, securities sales and trading, asset management, and commodities/derivatives trading. American Express ended 1996 at $56 up 37%. Lehman finished the year at 31 ⅜ up 48%.

Parent	Spin-Off	Spin-Off Date
AMR Corporation (AMR)	Sabre Reservations System (TSG)	10/10/96

AMR Corp., parent of American Airlines, recently spun-off approximately 20% of its Sabre Group Holdings in a initial public offering. The offer was priced at $27 a share and raised

$436 million. Sabre is the nation's largest computerized reservation service, processing 40% of all airline bookings made by travel agencies. Sabre became an independent, but wholly owned, company in June 1996. AMR is trying to highlight the hidden value in the reservations and consulting unit (and in the process enhance the value of its own stock) by floating 20% of Sabre to the public. This may be step one in an effort to facilitate a full-blown spin-off at a later date. Prior to the partial spin-off, Sabre was hidden in the belly of AMR, and consequently those assets were assigned an "airline" P/E multiple of around 10 times earnings. Clearly, AMR feels this unit will command a premium multiple (any multiple greater than AMR's current P/E will enhance stockholder value), as the market assigns a value more in line with other information-services companies. I would expect Sabre to be well received by the markets, as the only publicly traded airline reservation system. Sabre, which is about 20 years old, is one of the 10 largest computer service companies in terms of market capitalization. It is also the largest electronic distributor of travel data in the United States and processes 93 million requests for information per day.

Parent	Spin-Off	Spin-Off Date
Anheuser-Busch (BUD)	Earthgrains (EGR)	3/27/96

Anheuser-Busch, Inc., the world's largest brewer, announced on July 26th, 1995, its intentions to spin-off Earthgrains (formally called Campbell Taggert), its baking unit. Shareholders of record on March 19, 1996, received one share of Earthgrains for every 25 shares of Anheuser owned. Earthgrains is the third largest producer of packaged bakery products in the United States, including fresh, refrigerated, and frozen baked goods and refrigerated and frozen dough products. Its major fresh-bread brands in the United States include Colonial, Rainbo, IronKids, Grant's Farms, and Earthgrains.

Earthgrains is a good example of a spin-off that offered an excellent opportunity to buy shares at bargain-basement prices. The perception at the time of the divestiture was that the only reason Anheuser-Busch was spinning off Earthgrains was that nobody would buy the baking unit, which had no profit margin. At the same time, grain commodity prices were trading at levels not seen in many years. This backdrop was not conducive to getting Earthgrains sponsorship in the equity market. In fact, the stock traded in the mid-20s before settling into the low 30s for a long time. This price represented a deep discount to the tangible book value of $47 a share. Astute investors accumulated shares and were well rewarded as the stock lifted into the $50 range within six months of the spin-off. What was the catalyst in getting the stock moving? Earthgrains reported a blowout second quarter that was driven by cost cutting and strong pricing. Investors smelled a turnaround in earnings and bid up the shares. Interestingly, not a single analyst was recommending the stock after the spin-off. Earthgrains closed 1996 at $52 ¼, an increase of 87% since the March spin-off.

Parent	Spin-Off	Spin-Off Date
AT&T Corporation (T)	Lucent Technologies (LU)	9/30/96

On September 20, 1995, AT&T announced its historic plan to restructure the company into three independent companies via a spin-off of its communications equipment business (Lucent Technologies) and Global Information Services (now renamed NCR Corp.). AT&T offered an IPO of 15% of Lucent in the first quarter of 1996 (at $27 a share), with the spin-off of the remaining shares occurring in Fall 1996. AT&T Communications provides domestic and international communication services and products to business and residential customers. GIS is comprised primarily of AT&T's 1991 acquisition of computer manufacturer and distributor NCR. AT&T shareholders of record on September 17, 1996, received a stock dividend of Lucent on September 30 on the basis of approximately .326 of a share. Lucent closed 1996 at $46 ¼ a share, for a whopping 70% gain since its IPO, which was the largest ever U.S. history.

Parent	Spin-Off	Spin-Off Date
AT&T (T)	NCR (NCR)	1/2/97

AT&T finished its strategic restructuring by spinning off NCR to shareholders in a tax-free distribution. Shareholders received one share of NCR for every 16 shares of AT&T owned. On Wednesday, December 11, 1996, NCR Corp. shares were up significantly in "when-issued" trading on the NYSE. The first day the stock's value was recorded, it rose to 36 ¼ from 30 ⅞. Institutional investors liked the fact that NCR had moved into the black in the first nine months of 1996. NCR shares were distributed on December 31, 1996, to AT&T shareholders of record on December 13, 1996. So, for example, if you owned 100 shares of AT&T stock on December 13, 1996, you received an allotment of 6.25 shares of NCR common stock. The NCR distribution was tax-free to AT&T shareholders for federal income tax purposes.

Dayton-based NCR, formerly National Cash Register, makes computer systems and automated teller machines. AT&T bought NCR in 1991 for $7.5 billion in a hostile takeover, but the anticipated convergence of computers and telecommunications never emerged, and NCR fell into a cycle of slow sales and falling profits. In the first nine months of 1991, NCR had revenues of $4.3 billion with earnings of $63 million, but in the same period of 1995, it had losses of $501 million from revenues of $5.89 billion.

The takeover of NCR has been a debacle for AT&T. NCR has lost $4 billion since 1991, and AT&T had pumped $2.8 billion into NCR since 1993. Chairman and CEO Lars Nyberg, who took the helm at NCR in June, 1995, after 21 years at Dutch giant Phillips Electronics, may have the turnaround in hand. For instance, its workforce had been pared from 55,000 in 1991 to 39,000 today. Losses are narrowing. NCR expects second quarter 1997 per share results to be an improvement from 1996, when there was a loss of $18 million ($.18 per share). The company has all but left the PC business and closed several plants. NCR has refocused on the banking and retailing industries and will attempt to solidify its position as the world's leading seller of automatic teller machines for banks. The company is also a major supplier of cash registers, computers, and other equipment to customers in more than 130 countries.

The spin-off of NCR as a separate entity was the final phase in one of the largest corporate restructurings in history. The spin-off marked the completion of AT&T's restructuring announcement of September 20, 1995.

Parent	Spin-Off	Spin-Off Date
Ball Corporation (BLL)	Alltrista Corporation (JARS)	4/6/93

Alltrista Corporation is a manufacturer of food containers and industrial components.

Shareholders of record received one share of Alltrista for every four shares of Ball Corp. owned. Alltrista's food container products include Ball home-canning jars and other canning products. Muncie, Indiana-based Ball manufactures packaging products for food and beverages and provides aerospace and communication systems for government and commercial services.

Parent	Spin-Off	Spin-Off Date
Baxter International (BAX)	Caremark Int'l (CK)	12/2/92

Baxter spun off to its shareholders Caremark International in a tax-free divestiture, initiating a series of restructuring moves by the company. Baxter has become more focused on shareholder value. Nonstrategic assets have been sold, with the proceeds being used to buy back company stock. Shareholders received one share of Caremark for every four shares of Baxter owned. Caremark provides alternative-site patient care and managed-care services. Services include infusion therapy, hemophilia, and immune-deficiency therapy. The company's managed care business provides prescription-drug benefit program services. Caremark agreed to be acquired by Medpartners/Mullikin in 1996.

Parent	Spin-Off	Spin-Off Date
Baxter International (BAX)	Allegiance (AEH)	10/1/96

Baxter International Inc. spun off its $5 billion revenue hospital and surgical supply business to shareholders as an independent company. Shareholders received one share of Allegiance for every five shares of Baxter owned. Baxter's high-margin specialty division had little to do with its low-margin distribution business. This divestiture substantially represents a reversal of Baxter's 1985 acquisition of American Hospital Supply. Allegiance (the hospital supply operations) distributes more than 200,000 different items, including bandages, fluid collection devices, intravenous solution, and surgical instruments. The company sells its products through a direct salesforce and distributes to healthcare professionals and institutions in the United States and abroad.

Allegiance has performed very well since trading on its own since October 1996. AEH soared 70%, to close 1996 at 27 ⅝ in just three months since the divestiture.

Baxter consists of five more rapidly growing divisions: renal therapy, cardiovascular, biotechnology, intravenous therapy, and international hospitals. The purpose of the spin-off is to separate Baxter's mature, low-margin, low-growth hospital supply business from the faster growing and higher margin medical products businesses. The spin-off should enable Baxter to grow revenues and earnings at a double-digit rate.

Parent	Spin-Off	Spin-Off Date
Briggs & Stratton (BGG)	Strattec Security (STRT)	2/28/95

Briggs & Stratton spun-off Strattec Security, which manufactures locks for use in automobiles and other products. Milwaukee-based Strattec is the world's largest manufacturer of locks and keys for automobiles. The distribution ratio was one share of Strattec for every five shares of Briggs & Stratton. The purpose of the spin-off was to enable Strattec to pursue business strategies and objectives tailored to its unique financial and operating requirements as a manufacturer of mechanical and electromechanical locks and related prod-ucts. Briggs & Stratton management believed that the mar-ket value of Strattec was not reflected in the market price of Briggs & Stratton common stock prior to the spin-off and that the spin-off would highlight the hidden value.

Parent	Spin-Off	Spin-Off Date
Burlington Resources (BR)	El Paso Natural Gas (EPG)	7/1/92

In May 1992, Burlington Resources announced its intention to spin-off El Paso Natural Gas to stockholders. El Paso trans-ports, purchases, and sells natural gas. EPG owns and oper-ates an integrated, interstate natural gas pipeline system of approximately 17,000 miles, connecting supply regions in New Mexico, Texas, Oklahoma, and Colorado to markets in California, Nevada, Arizona, New Mexico, and Texas. One share of El Paso was distributed for every 4.177 shares of Burlington Resources.

On March 12, 1992, 5.75 million shares, or 15%, of EPG common stock was sold in an initial public offering at $19 per share. Burlington Resources is a diversified energy and natural resources holding company. Meridian Oil, a subsid-iary, explores for and develops oil and gas reserves.

Parent	Spin-Off	Spin-Off Date
Caliber System, Inc. (CBB)	Roadway Express (ROAD)	1/16/96

Roadway Express, Inc. was spun off of Caliber System, Inc. on January 2, 1996. When-issued trading in ROAD began January 2, 1996 at $17 per share. Caliber Systems (formerly called Roadway Services) shareholders received one share of Roadway Express for every two shares of CBB owned as of the record date December 29, 1995.

Stock in Caliber Systems surged after it announced plans to spin-off its Roadway Express trucking business, creating a separate, public company. Investors drove the stock up 4 ⅜, or 9%, to $55 ½, feeling that the operations would be more profitable apart than together. Analysts supported the move, which separates union-dominated ROAD from the mostly nonunion package delivery operation.

Akron, Ohio–based Caliber Systems was created when Roadway Services changed its name to Caliber System and spun-off its nationwide less-than-truckload (that is, less than 10,000 pounds) unit. Caliber retained 5% ownership of Roadway Express. Caliber Systems provides transportation (trucking) and logistics (delivery) businesses through its subsidiaries. The company's Roadway Package System subsidiary transports small packages. Roadway Regional Group (a subsidiary) is the parent company of Coles Express, Spartan Express, Central Freight Lines, and Viking Freight.

Roadway Express provides less-than-truckload, general-commodity freight carrier services to North and South America, Europe, Asia, and Australia. The company has closed over 130 terminals since 1995 and plans to shut down 40 facilities by the second quarter of 1997.

These moves to increase efficiency are paying off. The company should emerge into 1997 with profitability, no small feat for a unionized, long-haul LTL carrier. ROAD is challenged by the changing dynamics in the freight market. The less-than-truckload segment of the freight transportation is losing market share to other modes of transportation that are either faster or cheaper at moving freight, such as truckload, parcel, airfreight, and nonunion

Parent	Spin-Off	Spin-Off Date
Ceridian Corporation (CEN)	Control Data (CDAT)	9/1/92

Although possessing a history that goes back over 35 years, Control Data Systems was established in its current form in August 1992, when Ceridian Corporation transferred its Computer Products business to the company and subsequently distributed the firm's common stock to Ceridian's stockholders as a dividend (terms: 1:4 CEN).

Control Data Systems, Inc. helps large organizations develop the enterprisewide systems needed to create, transmit, access, and control business information. The company provides software and services focused on the architecture, implementation, and lifetime support of enterprise integration solutions for industry and government. The company is headquartered in Arden Hills, Minnesota. For 1995, Control Data reported net earnings of $8.9 million on revenues of $454.8 million.

The former parent, Ceridian, primarily is an information services and defense electronics company. The information services unit collects and analyzes data and delivers the results to customers. Its payroll employer-services division offers payroll and payroll-related services, human resource information, and benefit management services. Its Arbitron subsidiary estimates audience size and demographics for radio stations and advertising agencies.

Parent	Spin-Off	Spin-Off Date
Commercial Intertech (TEC)	CUNO (CUNO)	9/11/96

On July 29, 1996, Youngstown, Ohio–based Commercial Intertech (NYSE: TEC) declared a dividend to Commercial Intertech common shareholders of 100% of common stock of CUNO Inc., its fluid filtration and purification subsidiary. The CUNO shares were distributed on the basis of one common share of CUNO for each Commercial Intertech share outstanding, paid to holders of record as of the close of business on August 9, 1996.

Commercial Intertech manufactures industrial equipment. The company makes hydraulic components such as gear motors and telescopic cylinders, which are used mainly in construction and mining equipment. The Astron division makes metal buildings for use as aircraft hangers, athletic facilities, auto showrooms, supermarkets, and factories. The spin-off of CUNO, its most promising segment, leaves Commercial Intertech with more modest growth prospects going forward.

Commercial Intertech spun-off its high-growth subsidiary, CUNO, to prevent a hostile takeover attempt. Union Dominion, a diversified manufacturer of industrial and building products, bid $27 per share for TEC in June 1996. This was approximately 40% higher than Commercial Intertech's stock price at the time. TEC's management vigorously resisted the unsolicited tender offer, which they considered inadequate. Following the July announcement of the CUNO spinoff, Union Dominion backed away.

CUNO is headquartered in Meriden, Connecticut, and has eight manufacturing facilities in six countries. CUNO offers a full range of filtration and purification products to remove unwanted contaminants from fluids and gasses to three major market segments, including healthcare, fluid processing, and potable water. The spin-off was designed to unlock value for Commercial Intertech shareholders and ensure that shareholders rather than United Dominion realize the benefits of CUNO's leading position in the worldwide filtration business. In addition, management believed that the separation would provide shareholders with a stock multiple valuation for CUNO.

CUNO's comprehensive line of filtration products, most of which are disposable, effectively remove contaminants that range in size from molecules to sand particles. The companies sales are balanced between international and domestic markets. Significant customers include Boston Chicken, Kentucky Fried Chicken, McDonalds, Monsanto, and 3M. The spin-off should enhance CUNO's ability to acquire other companies in the filtration industry with common stock. In the past, such acquisitions were more difficult because its potential targets did not desire to hold Commercial Intertech common shares. The distribution should also enable shareholders to benefit from a higher growth rate of the CUNO business relative to Commercial Intertech's remaining businesses. The higher growth rates should translate into higher P/E multiples for the common shares.

Parent	Spin-Off	Spin-Off Date
Cole Taylor Financial (CTFG)	Cole Taylor Bank (RACC)	2/12/97

On November 15, 1996, Cole Taylor Financial Group, Inc. (NASDAQ: CTFG) announced shareholder approval of the previously proposed split-off of Cole Taylor Bank to a private investor group led by members of the Taylor family.

After the split, Cole Taylor Financial will change its name to
Reliance Acceptance Group Inc. to reflect its ongoing business of acquiring and servicing sales finance contracts, primarily in connection with the sale of used automobiles
through its Reliance Acceptance Corporation subsidiary. Prior
to the split-off, Cole Taylor Financial Group was the holding
company for Cole Taylor Bank, Reliance Acceptance Corp.,
and CT mortgage. The bank operates 10 offices in the Chicago area. Reliance's finance division finances automobiles
through 47 branch offices located in 16 states.

The transaction will enable the holding company to focus exclusively on the subprime automobile finance business.
Operating as Reliance Acceptance Corp., the auto finance
subsidiary has demonstrated substantial growth rates in earnings and assets since its incorporation as a separate operation in 1992. The nontaxable transaction created both a pure
play investment in the subprime auto finance industry and
the Chicago area's largest privately held bank. Under the
terms of the agreement, the holding company will receive
4.5 million shares of Cole Taylor Financial Group stock from
the Taylor group, plus the transfer from the bank of its automobile receivables business, principally consisting of cash
(about $50 million) and sales finance receivables, secured by
automobiles.

Parent	Spin-Off	Spin-Off Date
Cooper Industries (CBE)	Gardner-Denver Machinery, Inc. (GDMI)	4/25/94

Cooper Industries spun-off its Gardner-Denver Machinery
division to shareholders in a tax-free distribution of one share
GDMI for every 25 shares of CBE. Gardner Denver Machinery primarily manufactures air compressors and blowers for
various industrial applications, as well as petroleum pumps
and equipment used in oil and gas production and well servicing, drilling, and stimulation. Cooper Industries acquired
Gardner-Denver in 1979 and was split into a number of divisions. In 1985, several divisions were consolidated to form the
Gardner-Denver Industrial Machinery Division. In October

1993, Cooper Industries announced the spin-off of GDMI to Cooper's common shareholders in a tax-free transaction. Quincy, Illinois–based GDMI has been a stellar spin-off, having tripled in value over a two-and-a-half-year period since the divestiture. Even so, GDMI may have its best days ahead of it. With a market capitalization of $150 million it appears cheap relative to earnings and cash flow. GDMI has turned in a string of positive earnings comparisons since becoming a publicly traded company . Two recent acquisitions, a recovery in the petroleum equipment market, and healthy fundamentals for compressed air products should enable earnings growth at Gardner-Denver to continue through the next several years. In December 1996, GDMI announced a two-for-one stock split, with one additional share of common stock to be issued January 15, 1997 for every share held by shareholders as of record date on December 27, 1996. The split will increase the amount of common stock outstanding to approximately 9.9 million. This will enhance the liquidity of GDMI and make it easier for institutions to participate in the stock.

GDMI was a home-run in 1996, closing at $34 ¼ for a 80% return.

Parent	Spin-Off	Spin-Off Date
Corning (GLW)	Quest Diagnostics (DGX) Covance (CVD)	1/13/97

On May 14, 1996, Corning Inc. announced its plan to spin-off its clinical lab business as well as its pharmaceutical testing unit to shareholders, creating two additional, independent companies. Under the terms of the distribution, Corning Shareholders received one share of Quest Diagnostics, formerly known as Corning Clinical Laboratories Inc., for every eight common Corning shares held on the December 31 record date. Shareholders also received one share of Covance, formerly known as Corning Pharmaceutical Services, for every four common Corning shares held. This resulted in the distribution of 28 million shares of Quest Diagnostics and 56 million shares of Covance to Corning shareholders. Corning management feels that the companies will be valued more highly as independent entities, asserting that the "sum of the parts is worth more than the whole." Corning's stock has languished for nearly five years and is using a tax-free spin-off to shareholders as a way to dispose of a struggling business, focus on core operations, and boost shareholder value. Some businesses will remain with Corning, resulting in three separate, publicly traded companies. These lines include pollution-control devices, plastics, housewares, and fiber-optic cables, among others. Corning manufactures products made from specialty glass and related inorganic material. The company makes about 60,000 different products, most sold under the brand names of Corning, Corning Ware, Celcor, Corelle, and Pyrex. The spin-offs will allow Corning to focus on its specialty materials and communications businesses while allowing the two new companies to pursue their independent strategies more effectively.

Quest Diagnostics, headquartered in Teterboro, New Jersey, is one of the largest clinical laboratories in the country. Quest performs medical tests for healthcare providers. It performs its tests in 17 regional labs and 14 smaller branch labs across the United States and in a branch lab in Mexico City. The tests it performs on human tissue and fluids help doctors and hospital diagnose, treat, and monitor diseases from AIDS to cancer. Quest Diagnostics 18,700 employees process and provide data on more than 60 million specimens annually. Its center for research and development, Nichols Institute, develops and uses specialty tests utilizing advanced technology in such fields as endocrinology, oncology, and genetic testing. The competitive dynamics facing the clinical lab business (due to managed care) have placed significant pricing pressures on the industry, and I would not expect the market to be very interested in this business initially.

The outlooks for Corning and Covance are strong for the future. Covance, headquartered in Princeton, New Jersey, is one of the largest and most comprehensive biopharmaceutical development service companies in the world. Covance had annual revenues in 1995 of more than $400 million, operations in 15 countries, and over 5,000 employees worldwide. Covance provides preclinical services, health economics and outcomes research, central laboratory services, biotechnology manufacturing, pharmaceutical packaging services, clinical, and research products to pharmaceutical, biotechnology, and medical-device companies.

Corning's remaining businesses manufacture optical fiber, cable and components, high-performance glass and components for televisions, and other electronic displays for communications and communications-related industries; advanced materials for the scientific, life sciences, and environmental markets; and consumer products. Corning's total revenues from continuing operations in 1995 were $3.3 billion.

It is likely that the values of the three new entities will offer greater appreciation opportunities than the pieces combined. Corning's remaining businesses, with 20% growth in earnings, 20% plus returns, leadership, and dominant positions in its markets, should sell at a premium to the averages. The pharmaceutical services business is also the leader in a rapidly growing industry. As the company burns off its "conglomerate discount," I would expect the total value of the three separate businesses to surpass $50 a share.

Parent	Spin-Off	Spin-Off Date
Cyprus Amax Minerals Co., Inc. (CYM)	Alumax Inc. (AMX)	11/17/93

Amax Minerals spun-off its aluminum business, Alumax Inc., to shareholders on a ratio of one AMX for two CYM shares. Alumax is currently the fourth-largest aluminum producer in the country. Alumax produces and markets primary aluminum ingot and billet and fabricates value-added aluminum products used in the building, transportation, construction, and packaging industries. Separately, Amax merged with Cyprus Minerals and is trading under the name Cyprus Amax Minerals (CYM).

Cyprus Amax Minerals is a diversified mining company that produces copper, molybdenum, coal, and lithium.

Parent	Spin-Off	Spin-Off Date
Data Translation (DATX)	Media 100 (MDEA)	12/16/96

On July 30, 1996, Data Translation, Inc. announced plans to separate its Media 100 digital media group from its data acquisition and imaging and networking distribution business units. The company spun-off the data acquisition and imaging businesses in the form of a dividend and continues to operate the Media 100 business. Data Translation spun-off one share of common stock of its wholly owned subsidiary, Data Translation II, Inc. (New DTT) for every four shares of common stock of Data Translation, Inc. to its stockholders of record on November 29, 1996. The company with the spin-off changed its name to Media 100 Inc., reflecting its sole focus on its retained business and, on December 3, 1996, started trading under the MDEA ticker symbol. New DTI changed its name to Data Translation, Inc. and will trade under DATX.

The primary motivation behind the restructuring is to enable management to focus more exclusively on the high-growth Media 100 business. Media 100 is a complete video editing system, sold through a network of dealers to corporations, institutions, and professionals for use in creating training videos, educational programs, advertising, and other forms of video programming. It combines hardware and software to let business and creative professionals create finished videos. Media 100 is targeted to low-end broadcast video and 50,000-plus nonbroadcast video and advanced multimedia production sites in the United States alone. Since 1993, the company has sold over 5,000 systems. Media 100 takes source video information and digitizes it. Media 100 has accounted for almost all of the company's growth over the past several years. By committing to an open standard and continuous development of a complete range of software options and upgrades, the company believes that it is well positioned to continue to be a leader in its market. The company's other businesses, data acquisition and networking equipment distribution, have not performed well and have diluted the value of Media 100.

Parent	Spin-Off	Spin-Off Date
VIAD Corporation (VVI)	DIAL Corporation (DL)	8/16/96

Viad Corp., formerly known as Dial Corp., changed its name following the August 15, 1996 spin-off of its consumer products businesses (now known as Dial Corporation). Shareholders received one share of Dial Corporation stock for each share of Viad stock owned. On February 15, 1996, Dial Corp. announced plans to split the company into two major divisions: A consumer products company (DL) and a services company renamed Viad Corp. (VVI). Both companies started trading on the New York Stock Exchange as independent companies, and both were added to the S&P Midcap 400 index. Splitting the company was yet another step in the company's longtime restructuring, from a sprawling conglomerate involved in 20 different businesses into two, more focused, independent companies. The spin-off was intended to allow the services business group to pursue acquisition opportunities and help remove the conglomerate's disparate business lines.

The new Dial Corp. will consist of its consumer products businesses, comprised of four major product categories that the company manufactures and markets: skin care (soaps, antiperspirant, and hair care products); laundry (detergents, fabric softeners); household (air fresheners, cleaners, and other household items); and food (Armour Star chili, beef stew, corned beef hash, and other canned and packaged goods).

Dial Consumer Products originally began as the grocery food products division of Armour and Company, which was purchased by Dial's predecessor in 1970. Included in the acquisition was the brand name Dial, which is well-known worldwide. In 1983, Dial sold the Armour Food Company but retained the Dial brand name and certain canned meat lines. In recent years, acquisitions have added Purex household and industrial specialty products (1985), Borax household products (1988), Renuzit air fresheners (1993), and other consumer products. While Dial's consumer products domestic markets are mature, international sales should increase as management plans to emphasize further geographic expansion, especially into Latin America.

Viad is a $2.3 billion corporation made up of service companies spanning diverse industries. Viad companies are leaders in their niche markets and are focused on the areas of convention and tradeshow services, airline services, payment services, and travel and leisure. The services businesses consist of three segments, described next.

Airline Catering and Services

Dial conducts airline catering, airline refueling, and other ground-handling operations through Dobbs International Services (acquired 1987) and Aircraft Services (acquired 1968). Dobbs International, which has been conducting airline catering services since 1941, became the nation's largest domestic in-flight caterer as a result of its 1994 acquisition from United Airlines of 15 in-flight catering kitchens at 12 domestic airports. Dobbs provides in-flight meals to more than 60 domestic and international airlines at 48 airports in the United States and five airports in foreign countries.

Convention Services

Viad's GES Exposition and Exhibitgroup companies provides services to the $1.6 billion trade show and convention industry. GES Exposition, the nation's leading supplier of convention services, provides decorating, exhibit preparation, installation, electrical, transportation, and management services for conventions and trade shows. Exhibitgroup is a leading designer and builder of convention exhibits and displays, with manufacturing facilities in seven U.S. cities. Exhibitgroup designs, builds, transports, and coordinates trade show displays and marketing programs.

Travelers Express

Travelers Express is the nation's leading issuer of money orders (250 million) and handles payment services for banks, financial institutions, credit unions, and utilities. The Travelers Express group of companies sells money orders to the public through approximately 44,000 agent locations in the United States and Puerto Rico and is the nation's leading issuer of money orders. The company also provides processing services for approximately 5,000 credit unions and other financial institutions that offer share drafts.

One catalyst for the spin-off was noted money manager Michael Price of Heine Securities, who accumulated roughly 10% of Dial and pushed management for divestiture. Some Wall Street participants feel Dial should have split the services further (a trivestiture) in order to unlock shareholder value. This indeed may still happen, as Dial's longtime chairman John Teets is a sizable shareholder (controlling two million shares) and will likely pursue a strategy that will enhance his own wealth as he approaches retirement age. Going forward, I believe the prospects are more favorable for Viad. The company throws off considerable free cash flow, which can be used to cut its debt or fund acquisitions.

Parent	Spin-Off	Spin-Off Date
Dole Food Company (DOL)	Castle & Cooke, Inc. (CCS)	1/4/95

Founded in Hawaii in 1851, Dole Food is the world's largest producer and marketer of fresh fruits and vegetables and also markets a growing line of packaged foods. It does business in more than 90 countries, distributing fresh bananas, pineapples, grapes, melons, kiwi, and other fruit, vegetables, and nuts. Castle & Cooke, Inc. is a developer of residential and commercial real estate in Hawaii, Bakersfield, California, and Sierra Vista, Arizona and owns and operates two of the world's highest rated resorts on the (nearly wholly owned) island of Lanai in Hawaii. The company is also involved with commercial development throughout the United States.

Each Dole shareholder received one share of Castle & Cooke common for every three shares of DOL held. Approximately 20 million shares of Castle were issued to Dole shareholders. When-issued trading in the shares of Castle & Cooke closed at $18 on December 27. The value of the CCS distribution was $5 ⅜ per DOL share based on the price on December 29. The distribution of CCS was not a Section 355 spin-off and DOL did not have any profits for 1995, so the distribution was not taxable.

The distribution separated Dole's real estate and resorts business from its food business. Management believes that the separation will enhance shareholder values over the long term by allowing Dole and Castle to concentrate on their respective businesses and by enabling the investment community to analyze more effectively the investment characteristics, performance, and future prospects of the two businesses. CCS had been a drag on Dole's earnings. In March 1993, Dole spun-off its home-building unit in a public offering, but the stock fell, and Dole bought it back in August 1994.

The spin-off has allowed Dole Food to achieve visibly higher operating performance. DOL had made an effort to shift from the commodity foods to more value-added food products (such as prepackaged salads). The benefits of these strategies have been masked by the low-yield, asset-intensive CCS real estate operations. The spin-off left Dole with a relatively clean balance sheet.

Parent	Spin-Off	Spin-Off Date
Dover Corp. (DOV)	DOVatron International (DOVT)	6/1/92

Dover spun-off Dover Electronics (renamed DOVatron International) to its shareholders based on a 1 to 10 ratio. DOVatron International is a contract maker of electronic components employing leading-edge surface mount and fine pitch process technology. The parent, Dover, is a widely diversified manufacturer, making equipment for industrial, commercial, and municipal customers. Its subsidiary, Dover Elevator International, operates eight companies that make, install, and service elevators. Dover's other subsidiaries make equipment: fluid-delivery systems, power generators, electronic components, and parking meters.

Parent	Spin-Off	Spin-Off Date
Dresser Industries (DI)	INDRESCO Inc. (ID)	8/24/92

Dresser Industries provides products and services to the petroleum industry.

It makes well-drilling bits and related oilfield equipment and provides pipe-coating and seismic resource-exploration services. The equipment division manufactures compressors, pumps, turbines, and generators that are sold for use in power generation and petroleum processing. The engineering services division provides engineering and construction services for aboveground, underground, and offshore projects.

INDRESCO, spun-off from Dresser Industries (terms: 1:5 DI) is a high-quality machinery company serving four major markets: mining and construction equipment, refractory products, pneumatic tools, and air systems.

Parent	Spin-Off	Spin-Off Date
Duff & Phelps Corp. (DUF)	Duff and Phelps Credit Rating Co. (DCR)	11/1/94

Chicago-based Duff & Phelps Credit Rating, spun from Duff & Phelps in a tax-free stock dividend (terms: 1:3 DUF). DCR issues credit ratings on taxable corporate bonds, commercial paper, certificates of deposit, and other fixed-income securities. DCR's strong franchise, attractive returns, and growth potential bode well for the company. The company appreciated 68% in 1996.

Duff & Phelps provides financial services to institutional, corporate, and individual clients. Its services includes investment management, M&A analysis, and other consulting services. DUF also provides equity research on more than 700 companies and manages fixed income portfolios.

Parent	Spin-Off	Spin-Off Date
Dun & Bradstreet (DNB)	AC Nielsen (ART) Cognizant (CZT)	11/1/96

Dun & Bradstreet Corp. announced its restructuring in January 1996. On November 1, 1996, DNB completed its strategic restructuring into three separate, publicly held companies, including the spin-offs of Cognizant Corp. (CZT) and AC Nielsen (ART). For every share of Dun & Bradstreet Corp. stock, shareholders received one common share of Cogni-

zant and one common share of AC Nielsen stock. By spinning-off these businesses, DNB hopes to create a nimbler,
more focused organization, one better able to make faster,
more responsive decisions.

The slimmed-down Dun & Bradstreet Corp. now consists of three well known companies: D & B, the world's leading provider of business-to-business intelligence; Moody's
Investor Service, a global leader in rating debt; and R. H.
Donnelley, a leader in Yellow Pages marketing and publishing. The "new" DNB will be a $2 billion corporation with
16,000 associates in 40 countries. DNB will remain in the S&P
500 Index.

Cognizant Corp., a marketing information and information technology services company based in Westport, Connecticut, will be added to the S&P 500. Cognizant will consist
of IMS International, a supplier of marketing information to
the healthcare industries; Nielsen Media, a leader in audience measurement services; and a majority interest in Gartner
Group, a technology-consulting firm. These are the more
dynamic growth businesses previously within DNB.

AC Nielsen is a leader in market research and will focus
on business information services in the consumer-packag-
ing goods industries. ART will start as a stand-alone, independent company with $1.3 billion revenue base. It remains
to be seen if ART has been unshackled or cast adrift. Former
parent DNB tolerated AC Nielsen's losses to the tune of more
than $470 million in the three years prior to the spin-off. No
longer will the company be able to lean on Dun & Bradstreet.
AC Nielsen collects data from supermarket scanners and sells
it to customers, which use the information for corporate
analysis. It dominated this field until Chicago-based Information Resources Inc. (IRI) entered the field, initiating a harm-
ful price war. ART has seen its U.S. market share shrink to
48% in 1995 from 80% in the 1980s. Until the early 1990s,
Nielsen was the king of research. That changed when IRI won
over coveted customers like 3M and Georgia Pacific. They
were able to lure business away from Nielsen with intense
price cutting—sometimes as much as 30%. ART posted an
8% increase in third quarter (1996) revenues, to $347 million.
Earnings totaled $8.3 million, excluding tax benefits and

charges, versus a net loss of $9 million in the 1995 period. This represented a profit for the first time in four years. Nielsen's balance sheet looks adequate for the time being, with about $100 million in cash versus $40 million in debt as of November 1, 1996. Nielsen has a 30-person corporate staff based in Stamford, Connecticut, while 1,700 employees work at the operational headquarters in Schaumburg, Illinois, and another 15,000 are spread out over 88 countries. The stock started regular way trading November 4, 1996 at about $16 a share.

Parent	Spin-Off	Spin-Off Date
Eastman Kodak Co. (EK)	Eastman Chemical Company (EMN)	1/3/94

Shareholders received one share of Eastman Chemical for every four shares of Eastman Kodak owned. Eastman Chemical is a leading international chemical company with a broad portfolio of plastic, chemical, and fiber products. Its products are plastics used in soft-drink containers and plastic packaging, raw materials for coatings and paints, photographic chemicals, and engineered and compound plastics. The industrial products include fibers used in cigarette filters, intermediate chemicals, plastics used for packaging, and yarns used in the fabric industry.

Eastman Kodak Company is the world's largest producer of photographic products, making film, photographic plates, photographic chemicals, cameras and projectors, photographic plates, and processing equipment.

Parent	Spin-Off	Spin-Off Date
Eaton Vance Corp. (EV)	Investors Financial Services Corp. (IFIN)	11/11/95

Eaton Vance is an investment-management holding company that manages and markets mutual funds while providing management and counseling services to individuals and institutions. On November 10, 1995 EV Spun off its 77.3%

owned subsidiary, Investors Financial Services Corp. Shareholders received 2.812 shares of IFIN for every 10 EV held,
and 0.541 Class A for every 10 EV owned.

Investors Financial Services Corp. provides asset administration services to the financial services industry through
its wholly owned subsidiary, Investors Bank & Trust Company. Unlike traditional banks, IFIN does not focus on providing retail banking services. It has no retail branches, offers
no credit cards, and makes no small-business loans. Instead,
it provides asset administration services such as domestic
and global custody, multicurrency accounting, mutual fund
administration, institutional transfer agency, foreign exchange, securities lending, and portfolio performance measurement services. Its clients include a variety of financial
asset managers, including mutual fund complexes, investment advisors, banks, and insurance companies.

Investors Bank & Trust Company operated as a subsidiary of Eaton Vance from 1969 to 1995. In November 1995,
the business operations were spun-off to Eaton Vance shareholders. In addition, 2.3 million shares of IFIN common stock
were sold to the public in an initial public offering at $16 ½
(raising $34 million) that closed November 13, 1995. The prin-
cipal reason for the spin-off was to eliminate restrictions im-
posed on IFIN so that EV would not be regulated as a bank
holding company. Since the enactment of the Competitive
Equality Banking Act (CEBA), IFIN's asset growth had been
restricted to an annual cap of 7%. As a result of the spin-off,
the company has been able to expand its business activities.
Prior to the IPO and concurrent spin-off from Eaton Vance,
IFIN was limited in its ability to grow its balance sheet assets
by CEBA restrictions. Now the CEBA restrictions no longer
apply, IFIN can capture its off-balance-sheet deposits and expand its assets to a level consistent with its capital position.
Freedom from the CEBA restrictions has enabled the bank to
grow its assets from $187 million at October 31, 1995 to $759
million at June 30, 1996.

Freed from CEBA restrictions, IFIN is now in a position
to undertake new business opportunities. In particular, it is
in a position to bring onto its balance sheet various client

deposits which it had been directing to other financial institutions because of CEBA-imposed regulations. IFIN finished 1996 up 34%. EV surged 69%.

Parent	Spin-Off	Spin-Off Date
Emulex Corp. (EMLX)	Qlogic (QLGC)	2/28/94

One share of Qlogic was spun-off to shareholders for every one share of Emulex Corp. owned. QLogic supplies semiconductor chips that connect peripheral devices to computer systems. The firm also provides chips that direct the flow of data at high speeds between multiple computers and such peripheral devices as tape drives, scanners, printers, and CD-ROMs. International sales comprise approximately two-thirds of revenues.

Emulex provides connectivity solutions to users of local area networks and wide area networks. The company designs network-communication products, including servers, software, and wide-area network adapters. Qlogic was a big winner in 1996. The company surged 238% and closed at $25 ¾ a share. Emulex too had market-beating returns, up 54% in 1996.

Parent	Spin-Off	Spin-Off Date
Ethyl Corp. (EY)	Albemarle (ALB)	3/11/93

Ethyl spun-off the company's industrial chemicals operations to shareholders on a one-for-two ratio. Ethyl manufactures chemicals used in petroleum and industrial products, primarily petroleum additives for gasoline and diesel fuels, hydraulic fluids, lubricants, and automatic-transmission fluids. Ethyl spun-off Albemarle, the company's industrial chemicals operations, which included Olefins and Derivatives, Specialty Chemicals, and Bromine Chemicals. The company's products include chemicals for polymers, detergents, personal-care products, pharmaceuticals, and petroleum applications. Albemarle's chemicals are used in plastics, insulation, soaps, bleaches, lubricants, pesticides, analgesics, herbicides, and fungicides.

Parent	Spin-Off	Spin-Off Date
First Mississippi Corp. (FRM)	FirstMiss Gold (GGO)	10/20/95

On May 2, 1995, First Mississippi announced the distribution of its 81% interest in its publicly traded subsidiary, FirstMiss Gold, in a tax-free distribution. On October 20, FRM completed the spin-off of FirstMiss Gold to FRM shareholders with a distribution of 14.75 million shares of stock with a market value of $313 million, or $15 per FRM share. The spin-off ratio was .70846 shares of FirstMiss Gold for every 1 share of FRM owned. The purpose of the spin-off was to highlight the value of the mining assets. In May 1996, FirstMiss Gold changed its name to Getchell Gold (GGO) and started trading on the American Stock Exchange. FirstMiss Gold, now known as Getchell Gold, went public in May 1988 when FRM sold 19% of the company. After the spin-off, FRM and GGO were sold off due to structural selling by index funds. Standard & Poor's moved First Mississippi from its S&P 500 Index to its Small Cap 600 Index at spin-off. As a result, there was substantial selling by index funds, which have approximately $320 billion invested in the S&P 500, and relatively little buying by index funds, which have about $500 million in the Small Cap 600.

First Mississippi Corp. (FRM) consists of three primary operating divisions: Chemicals, Fertilizers, and Combustion & Thermal Plasma. The company produces chemicals that include aniline, ammonia, nitrotolulene, and urea used by the fertilizer industry.

Parent	Spin-Off	Spin-Off Date
First Mississippi Corp. (FRM)	"Fertilizer Operations"	1/6/97

First Mississippi Corp. produces chemicals for industry and agriculture and related products and services. First Mississippi Corp. announced further restructuring on August 28,

1996. FRM's board of directors approved the disposition of the company's fertilizer operations via a merger with Mississippi Chemical Corp. (NASDAQ: GRO). The transaction, utilizing the structure commonly referred to as a Morris Trust, occurred in two steps: First, the tax-free spin-off to shareholders of the company's chemicals and related businesses in the form of a new, publicly traded company that retained the First Mississippi name; and second, the tax-free merger of the company's remaining fertilizer operations with Mississippi Chemical. First Mississippi shareholders received approximately 6.9 million shares of Mississippi Chemical stock, or 0.335 shares of Mississippi Chemical stock for each share of First Mississippi stock. First Mississippi's debt will be assumed by First Mississippi Chemical in the merger. Cash on hand (estimated between $50 to $60 million) will be transferred to the spun-off chemical company, which will be debt free. Management believes the "prospects for continued growth in chemicals revenues and earnings are good" and that the "combined value of the chemicals business and the stock of Mississippi Chemical received by shareholders will exceed the value of First Mississippi alone as presently structured." First Mississippi's fiscal 1996 fertilizer operating profits were $65.8 million on sales of $224 million.

Parent	Spin-Off	Spin-Off Date
Florida Progress Corp. (FPC)	Progress Credit Corp. (EIN)	12/18/96

On November 21, 1996, Florida Progress (NYSE: FPC) approved the previously announced spin-off of Echelon International Corporation (NYSE: EIN), its lending, leasing, and real estate company, to shareholders. Each Florida Progress shareholder of record as of December 5, 1996 received 1 share of Echelon International for every 15 shares of Florida Progress. In July, FPC announced its decision to spin-off the lending, leasing, and real estate operations (renamed Echelon International) to its shareholders through a tax-free stock dividend. The purpose of the spin-off was to allow Florida Progress to focus its attention on its core utility and coal and transportation businesses. Florida Progress is a Fortune 500 diversified utility holding company with assets of $5.6 billion. Its principal subsidiary is Florida Power, the state's second largest electric utility, with about 1.3 million customers. Diversified operations include coal mining, marine operations, rail service, and life insurance. The utility operations are likely to benefit from more people and businesses relocating to Florida to take advantage of the state's climate and low tax structure.

Echelon is a real estate and financial services company with operations in two business segments: The real estate business and the lending and leasing business. Located in St. Petersburg, Florida, Echelon owns and manages a portfolio of income-producing commercial real estate properties located in Florida. The majority of these properties are located in the Tampa Bay area, including Tampa, St. Petersburg, and the Gateway area in between Tampa, St. Petersburg, and Clearwater. Echelon's owned assets include 11 major commercial real estate properties, consisting of 5 office buildings and 6 industrial sites, and other properties. EIN manages a portfolio of commercial real estate loans throughout the United States. The aggregate load balance as of September 30, 1996 was $97.2 million. The largest single geographic concentration of loans is in the state of Florida. The real estate portfolio consists of loans secured by a diverse group of properties, including single tenant and multitenant office buildings, life-care facilities, and industrial properties. In addition, EIN owns and manages a portfolio of leveraged, direct finance, and operating leases of aircraft and other equipment and a number of collateralized loans secured by aircraft. Echelon's portfolio of leveraged leases represent transactions in which Echelon acts as the equity investor and owner participant. Progress is trading around $15 a share.

Parent	Spin-Off	Spin-Off Date
Foothill Group (FGI)	Pacific Crest Capital (PCCI)	12/23/93

Foothill spun-off its thrift & loan subsidiary into the holding company Pacific Crest Capital. Shareholders received 1 share of PCCI for every 15 shares of FGI owned prior to the divestiture. Foothill Thrift is a California-licensed industrial loan company whose primary source of operating income is interest income from its commercial real estate mortgage portfolio.

Parent	Spin-Off	Spin-Off Date
General Mills (GIS)	Darden Restaurants (DRI)	6/1/95

General Mills produces a variety of packaged foods, including cereals, baking goods, snack foods, flour, yogurt, and beverages. In December 1994, the company announced its plan to separate into two, independent, public corporations—one for consumer foods and one for restaurants. In a tax-free transaction, General Mills shareholders received one share of Darden Restaurants for each share of General Mills owned. Management believes that separate corporations with highly integrated strategies and incentive programs will produce the strongest growth performance and enhance long-term shareholder value.

Orlando-based Darden Restaurants operates the nationwide casual dining restaurants Red Lobster and the Olive Garden. Red Lobster restaurants feature seafood; Olive Garden features an Italian theme. Recently, DRI introduced a new restaurant call Bahama Breeze, which offers Caribbean cuisine. Since the spin-off, Wall Street has been very skeptical of Darden due to the significant challenges the company faces in strengthening Red Lobster's sales and earnings. Tough competition and rapid expansion from other casual dining chains has left analysts with a degree of uncertainty regarding Darden's growth prospects going forward. DRI's management recently made some marketing changes in an effort to revitalize the tired Red Lobster theme. Red Lobster is dropping prices, adding new entrees, and increasing its portions. The chain of more than 600 restaurants is also committing $150 million to redecorate and more than 75% of its restaurants will have a "wharfside look" within the next year.

If Darden succeeds in pumping some life into Red Lobster, the stock may be an excellent value play. Currently, it trades at a modest multiple to its book value and throws off

good cash flow. Wall Street prognosticators are likely to ig-
nore DRI for more exciting, momentum-type themes (such
as Outback Steakhouse and Logan's Roadhouse for example)
until Darden can demonstrate a well-established turnaround.
Darden closed 1996 at $8 ¾ a share, down 26% in 1996—it
looks cheap at this level.

Parent	Spin-Off	Spin-Off Date
Getty Realty (GPM)	Getty Petroleum (GTY)	2/1/97

December 12, 1996, Getty Petroleum Corp. (NYSE: GTY) reported that the company's Board of Directors approved the
spin-off of the company's marketing business to its stockholders. Each shareholder received one share of stock in the
new company, Getty Petroleum Marketing Inc., for each share
of Getty Petroleum Corp. held as of January 31, 1997. At the
time of the distribution, Getty Petroleum Corp. changed its
name to Getty Realty Corp. The assets to be transferred to
Getty Petroleum Marketing Inc. include the company's marketing equipment, supply contracts, and working capital directly associated with the marketing and heating oil
businesses. Getty Realty Corp. would retain the company's
fee and leased properties, including service stations, supply
terminals, and the company's heating oil business.

Getty Petroleum Corp. markets petroleum products.
The company is one of the nation's largest marketers of gasoline and petroleum products, supplying approximately 1,600
branded locations in 12 Northeastern and Middle Atlantic
states, including approximately 1,100 owned or leased properties. GTY also markets heating oil and is a wholesale distributor of a variety of petroleum products through its East
Coast petroleum storage and distribution network.

Parent	Spin-Off	Spin-Off Date
H&R Block (HRB)	CompuServe (CSRV)	4/19/96

On February 20, 1996, H&R Block announced its intention
to divest CompuServe, its on-line services provider. The

company IPO'd 18.4 million shares of CompuServe, representing nearly 20% of its outstanding shares, to the public at $30 a share on April 19, 1996. The net proceeds of the IPO were $519 million. CompuServe repaid $205 million in debt to H&R Block. The company had intended to separate the companies within 12 months of the IPO, but in August 1996 announced that its Board of Directors decided not to present to shareholders the proposed spin-off of CompuServe at its September 11 annual meeting. The company has suspended the rest of the spin-off, citing CompuServe's performance and market conditions. CompuServe had announced a string of poor financial results due to the competitive environment facing the on-line/Internet access industry. Its stock had plummeted from a post-IPO high of $35 to below $10 as it struggled to retain customers. The Board continues to believe that a separation of CompuServe is in the best interests of H&R Block shareholders, but is waiting for implementation of CompuServe's newly announced business strategy (focusing on business and professional users rather than home users) to turn the company around before completing the spin-off.

Founded in 1955, H&R Block, Inc. is a diversified company offering tax, financial, and information services. H&R Block is the country's largest tax-preparation firm, servicing 17.4 million taxpayers in nearly 9,700 offices in the United States, Canada, Australia, and 15 other countries and territories. In the States, H&R Block Tax Services, Inc. handled approximately one in every seven returns filed with the IRS last year.

H&R Block paid $20 million for CompuServe in 1980. The sagging fortunes of CompuServe has weighed on H&R Block's performance. CompuServe lost $58 million in the second quarter ending October 31, 1996 and continues to lose market share to rival America On-Line. If CompuServe can find a way to stem customer defections, it may be an interesting speculation for the long haul. The hidden jewel in CompuServe's business is its Network Services Division, which provides private network and Internet services to major corporations. Visa transactions and Federal Express package-tracking are among the corporate activities conducted over the CompuServe network, which has posted consistent and impressive gains in revenues and profits over the past several years. This business is characterized by long-term contracts with major corporations. The key trend influencing the opportunities for CompuServe has been the rapid commercialization of the Internet over the past two years. The Internet, a worldwide electronic network, uses open computer communications standards and relatively inexpensive routers and servers over lines leased from telephone networks to connect millions of businesses and consumers worldwide, effectively connecting an increasingly disparate base of computer hardware and software operating systems ranging from PCs to supercomputers. This network technology, which historically had been used primarily by government and academic organizations globally, is rapidly being adopted by the private commercial market.

CompuServe closed 1996 at $9 ⅞ a share, down 66% from the IPO price of $30 in April 1996. H&R Block closed at $29 a share, well off its highs of nearly $50 a share.

Parent	Spin-Off	Spin-Off Date
Halliburton Co. (HAL)	Highland Insurance Services (HIC)	1/24/96

On October 11, 1995, Halliburton announced its plan to spin-off its Highlands Insurance subsidiary to shareholders via a tax-free distribution. Shareholders of record on January 4, 1996, received 1 share of HIC for every 10 shares of Halliburton owned. Highlands started trading in the when-issued market on January 11 around $22 a share.

Halliburton is one of the world's largest diversified-energy services, engineering, maintenance, and construction companies. Founded in 1919, Halliburton provides a broad range of energy services and products, industrial and marine engineering, and construction services. Halliburton provides technical and construction services, mainly to energy-related industries, and produces related products. The energy services subsidiary makes drilling equipment and provides maintenance, testing, and data-processing services for the petroleum industry. HAL's Engineering & Construction Services unit performs feasibility, design, engineering, and project and construction management services for the process and marine industries and hazardous waste sites.

Highlands Insurance Group is engaged in the commercial property and casualty insurance business. HIC's main product lines include worker's compensation insurance, general liability insurance, and commercial automobile-liability insurance.

In connection with the spin-off, Insurance Partners L.P. and management invested $60 million in Highlands in the form of convertible debt and warrants. Insurance Partners investment will allow it to acquire up to 43% of Highlands for a total investment of $130 million. Insurance Partners L.P. is a consortia of Centre Reinsurance Holdings (Zurich Insurance), Keystone Inc. (Robert Bass), and Chase Manhattan Corp. Highlands Insurance Services closed 1996 at around $20, down 10% from its initial when-issued price of $22 on January 11, 1996. The company is trading for roughly book value on a fully diluted basis. The company currently has no formal research coverage.

Parent	Spin-Off	Spin-Off Date
Hanson PLC (HAN)	U.S. Industries (USI)	5/31/95

U.S. Industries has been publicly traded since June 1, 1995, when it was spun-off from Hanson PLC. USI closed its first day of trading at $13 ¾. It is a diversified industrial management corporation. U.S. Industries is composed of 19 companies; 90% of its operating profit is derived from seven well-known, market-leading core businesses such as Jacuzzi, Ames garden tools, Ertl toys, Rexair vacuum cleaners, Lighting Corporation of America, EJ Footwear, Garden State Tanning, and Tommy Armour Golf. The spin-off enabled Hanson to efficiently divest 34 small U.S. companies in a tax-effective manner. Record and distribution dates were May 24 and May 31, respectively. The spin-off ratio was 1 USI share for every 20 Hanson ADRs.

U.S. Industries, Inc. (USI) is organized into three business segments: Consumer Group, Building Products Group, and Industrial Group. The Consumer Group is comprised of Ames, Rexair, Ertl, and EJ Footwear. Ames is a leading manufacturer and distributor of nonpowered lawn and garden tools. Rexair is the second largest manufacturer and distributor of premium vacuum cleaners and accessories (Rainbow). Ertl is the largest manufacturer of agricultural and miniature replica toys, model kits, and collectibles (AMT and ERTL Collectibles). EJ Footwear manufactures and imports a variety of footwear (Durango, Georgia Boot, Lehigh, and Baby Deer).

The Building Products Group is comprised of Jacuzzi and Lighting Corporation of America. Jacuzzi is the largest manufacturer of whirlpool bath spas, shower systems, and nonjetted baths. Lighting Corporation of America is the third-largest manufacturer of lighting fixtures in North America (including CPM, Kim, Spaulding, and Progress). The industrial Group is made up of Garden State Tanning, a leader in premium automotive leather seating.

USI stock has performed well since being spun-off from Hanson. The shares have more than doubled in the 18 months as a standalone public company, closing 1996 at $34 ⅝. USI has made considerable progress in reducing the debt that Hanson loaded them up with prior to the split. Net debt was reduced from $942 million at September 30, 1995 to $689 million in 1996. USI earned $1.81 per share from continuing operations, a 43% increase over the 1.27 reported in 1995 on an adjusted basis.

Parent	Spin-Off	Spin-Off Date
Hanson PLC (HAN)	Millennium Chemical (MCH)	10/2/96
	Imperial Tobacco (IMT.L)	10/1/96
	Energy	(Early 1997)

On January 30, 1996, Hanson PLC unveiled its plan to demerge into four publicly traded companies: energy, chemicals, tobacco, and building & equipment. The chemicals business is listed in New York, the tobacco business in London, energy in New York and London, and Hanson, the building materials business, also in New York and London. The British conglomerate announced plans to split into separately traded units as a way to boost shareholder value, but the financial community pushed Hanson shares significantly lower. The ADRs were trading at around $15 a share when the demerger was announced and crept continually lower as the spin-off approached. The split was panned by many analysts, who cited an increase in cost of capital and tax rate. Hanson executives see significant potential for earnings growth by all four new companies. Getting out from under the Hanson umbrella should allow them to focus on operations without struggling with competing agendas from headquarters.

Shareholders approved the breakup on September 25, 1996. Shares in Imperial Tobacco and Millennium Chemicals began trading independently of Hanson on October 1 and October 2, 1996, respectively. In early 1997, Hanson split-off its Energy Group, consisting of Peabody Coal Co. and Hanson's electricity-distribution businesses.

Distribution Ratios

One share of Millennium Chemicals was spun-off for every 70 Hanson ordinary shares (1 share of common stock for every 14 Hanson ADRs);1 Imperial Tobacco ordinary share for every 10 Hanson ordinary shares (1 ADR for every 4 Hanson ADRs); and 1 Energy Group ordinary share for every 10 Hanson ordinary shares (1 ordinary share for every 2 Hanson ADRs).

Hanson PLC had a history of buying undervalued companies, boosting results through streamlining, and selling with a solid profit. Lord Hanson and the late Lord White built Hanson by buying undervalued companies, then turning them around. With conglomerates very much out of favor in the investment community, and the stock slipping to seven-year lows, Hanson decided to demerge the company further, following the successful divestiture to U.S. Industries (USI). The USI spin-off demonstrated that increased focus works and such radical restructuring pays off.

The chemical unit consists of Quantum Chemical, SCM Chemicals, SCM Glidco Organics, and a 35% interest in Suburban Propane. Quantum Chemical, acquired in 1993 for $3.4 billion, is the largest U.S. producer of polyethylene, or plastic. Quantum is also a major producer of specialty polymers and industrial chemicals, including methanol, VAM, and acetic acid. SCM Chemicals is the world's third-largest producer of titanium dioxide—the whitening agent in paint, paper, and plastic. SCM Glidco Organics is a worldwide leader in the manufacture of fragrance and flavor ingredients.

The tobacco unit consists of Imperial Tobacco Limited. Imperial Tobacco, purchased in 1986, is the second-largest tobacco company in the United Kingdom, holding a 37% market share. Shares of this new company are traded in London.

The energy unit consists of Eastern Group PLC, Peabody Holding, and Peabody Resources (Australia). Peabody Holding Company, the largest U.S. producer of low-sulfur coal, produces more than 150 million tons of coal annually from 28 mines in the United States and three in Australia.

The New Hanson will consist of ARC Ltd., Cornerstone Construction, Grove Worldwide, Hanson Brick, Hanson Electrical and Hanson Property, 39% of RGC Ltd., and a 12.5% interest in the National Grid Group PLC. With the mix of cyclical and slow-growth assets, you would not expect Hanson to trade a premium earnings multiple. But the stock's current valuation seems unduly low at $7 per ADR.

Parent	Spin-Off	Spin-Off Date
Harcourt General Inc. (H)	GC Companies Inc. (GCX)	12/16/93

Harcourt General spun-off its General Cinema theater operations to stockholders in a tax-free dividend (terms: 1:10 H). GC Companies operates a chain of motion-picture theaters under the General Cinema Theaters name and exhibits films on a first-run basis. Almost one-third of the company's theaters are located in California, Florida, and Texas.

The company plans to open 17 new megaplex theaters with approximately 240 screens during the next three years, including 80 screens in fiscal 1997. Management's stated strategy is to build high-impact theaters in densely populated areas while divesting portfolio locations that no longer provide an adequate return. The aim is to improve cash flow margins and take advantage of attractive opportunities to invest new capital in the theater business. As of October 31, 1996, General Cinema operated 1,159 screens in 189 locations compared to 1,180 screens in 196 locations as of October 31, 1995. For the year ended October 31, 1996, GC Companies reported that net earnings increased 98.1% to $17.2 million, or $2.20 a share. Revenues for fiscal 1996 were $446 million, compared to $451.3 million in 1995.

Parent	Spin-Off	Spin-Off Date
Harris Corporation (HRS)	Harris Computer Systems (NHWK)	10/7/94

On June 26, 1996, Harris Computer Systems changed its name to CyberGuard Corporation. The stock symbol changed from NHWK to CYBG (NASDAQ). The name change reflects the company's commitment to the fast-growing network security market.

CyberGuard (formally Harris Computer Systems) was spun off from Harris Corporation in October 1994. Harris Computer Systems consisted of the Trusted Systems Division (now CyberGuard) and the Real-time Systems Division. The real-time computer business was sold to Concurrent Computer Corporation. CyberGuard designs, manufactures, and markets secure computing solutions, including operation systems, networking products, Internet/intranet firewalls, and consulting services. The tax-free spin-off gave shareholders one share of NHWK for every 20 shares owned. On March 7, 1996 CyberGuard declared a three-for-one stock split of CyberGuard's outstanding common stock for holders of record as of March 18. The split changed the number of shares outstanding to approximately 6 million. CYBG is currently number three in market share after Checkpoint and Secure Computing.

CyberGuard is a small-cap (under $100M) company with solid prospects as Internet use becomes more prevalent at work and home and the worldwide information security market blossoms. The stock hit a high in June 1996 of $25. Harris Corporation develops, designs, manufactures, markets, and services high-technology electronic systems, equipment, and components, such as communication systems for military and space programs, semiconductors, and communications equipment for the broadcast telecommunication industries. The Lanier Worldwide subsidiary makes office equipment, including copiers, dictation systems, and fax machines, as well as speech-recognition systems.

Parent	Spin-Off	Spin-Off Date
Home Shopping Network (HSN)	Precision Systems (PSYS)	8/17/92

St. Petersburg, Florida–based Precision Systems, Inc. develops and manufacturers integrated voice and call-processing systems. Precision was spun-off from HSN in August 1992 (terms: 1:10 HSN). Its systems provide voice-activated dialing, interactive voice response, custom message announcements, automated attendant, call routing, and other features. In addition, the company makes systems offering specialized fax services.

Parent	Spin-Off	Spin-Off Date
Home Shopping Network (HSN)	Silver King Communications (SKTV)	1/14/93

Home Shopping Network, Inc., is a holding company whose primary business is electronic retailing, conducted by its Home Shopping Club subsidiary. HSC sells consumer goods and services through live-broadcast, customer-interactive retail-sales programs which it transmits to TV stations, cable systems, and satellite-dish receivers.

Silver King, a spin-off from Home Shopping (terms: 1:1 HSN), owns and operates TV stations that primarily broadcast programming produced by the Home Shopping Club. The spin-off was initiated to facilitate investor understanding of Silver King's and Home Shopping Network's businesses, which management felt would result in greater value in the long term for HSN's shareholders.

Parent	Spin-Off	Spin-Off Date
Host Marriott Corp. (HMT)	Host Marriott Services (HMS)	2/2/96

Host Marriott Corporation was the name taken by Marriott Corporation when, through a special dividend, it split into two separate companies in October 1993. Host Marriott Corporation is one of the largest owners of lodging properties in the world, operated primarily under the Marriott brand names. Host Marriott Corporation will focus on its strategy of owning and acquiring full-service hotel properties based on their strategic alliance with Marriott International, Inc. In August 1995, the company announced its intention to divide its operations into two separate companies by divesting its concessions business, Host Marriott Services (terms: 1:5 HMT). The company should garner a higher multiple to cash flow valuation as a "pure" hotel company.

Headquartered in Bethesda, Maryland, Host Marriott Services Corporation (HMS) is the leading domestic operator of airport and toll-road food, beverage, and merchandise concessions. The company operates restaurants, gift shops, and related facilities at 71 airports, 90 travel plazas on 13 toll roads and at numerous tourist attractions, casinos, stadiums, and arenas. With revenues of $1.2 billion, Host Marriott Services is best known for its custom solutions business approach, which combines internationally known brands with regional favorites in airports, travel plazas, shopping malls, and sports and entertainment attractions. The company has a dominant market share in U.S. airports and significant growth potential in the following areas: international airport expansion; sports arena contracts; and increased merchandising opportunities at existing locations. HMS has consistently been able to generate strong operating cash flows and may consider alternative uses of cash, such as initiating an annual dividend or a stock buyback. HMS closed 1996 at $9 ¼, up 40% from its initial trading of $6 ½ in February of 1996.

Parent	Spin-Off	Spin-Off Date
Humana Inc. (HUM)	Galen Health Care, Inc.	3/8/93

On March 1, 1993, Humana separated into two, independent, publicly held companies. Humana retained the managed care health plan business. Humana, one of the nation's largest managed healthcare services companies, provides health-benefits plans for approximately three million subscribers. The company owns and manages HMOs and PPOs that provide services to members through 85,000 physicians. Humana spun-off its hospital operations into Galen Health Care (terms: 1:1 HUM), which was promptly acquired by Columbia Healthcare Corp. in September 1993. Humana was a good example of structural selling creating an excellent buying opportunity. As a result of the divestiture, Humana was dropped from the S&P 500 Index, which set off index fund selling. You could have bought all you wanted for around $6 a share. Humana subsequently tripled within a year.

Parent	Spin-Off	Spin-Off Date
Inland Steel, Inc. (IAD)	Ryerson Tull, Inc. (RT)	6/20/96

Chicago-based Inland Steel Industries, Inc. is a materials management, logistics, and technical-services company that provides value-added steel products and materials-related services to manufacturers in the automotive, appliance, furniture, equipment, electric motor, and other industries. Its three business units are Inland Steel company, the sixth-largest U.S. steel producer; Ryerson Tull, Inc., the largest U.S. metals and industrial plastics service center operation, comprised of Joseph T. Ryerson & Son. and J.M. Tull Metals Company, Inc.; and Inland International, Inc.

On May 7, 1996, Inland Steel Industries announced an initial public offering and note offering of its materials distribution subsidiary, Ryerson Tull, Inc. Inland Steel believes that the consummation of the IPO and note offering, which will establish public trading markets for the company's equity and debt securities and should provide RI with access to the public markets to raise additional capital to fund its future growth. Proceeds from the offering were used to retire Inland debt. Inland IPO'd a 15% interest in Ryerson Tull on June 20, 1996, at $16 a share. It is anticipated that a potential distribution of shares in a spin-off will occur at some point.

Ryerson Tull is a general-line metals service center and processor of metals. RT had 1995 sales of $2.5 billion and a current U.S. market share of approximately 9%. The company distributes and processes metals and other materials throughout the United States and is among the largest purchasers of steel in the country. Ryerson Tull also owns a 50% interest in Ryerson de Mexico, a general-line metals service center and processor with 18 facilities in Mexico.

Parent	Spin-Off	Spin-Off Date
Interco (ISS)	Converse (CVE)	11/18/94

Interco distributed all of the outstanding shares of Converse to holders of Interco in a tax-free distribution to shareholders as part of the company's 1994 "trivestiture." Interco separated the company into three publicly traded entities—Interco (ISS), Converse (CVE), and Florsheim Shoe (FLSC)—by means of a distribution of Converse and Florsheim to Interco shareholders.

Converse designs and manufactures athletic and leisure footwear and licenses sports apparel and accessories. The company has sold 560 million pairs of shoes worldwide. Shareholders received one share of Converse for every three shares of Interco owned. Interco loaded up Converse and Florsheim with substantial debt prior to the spin-off. CVE proceeded to make a number of strategic blunders that tarnished its image on Wall Street. The stock plummeted from near $12 a share after the spin-off to under $4 a share as the prospects dimmed. Ironically, Converse became the second-best performing company on the New York Stock Exchange, appreciating a mind-boggling 312% in 1996. CVE started the

year at $4 ⅛ and closed 1996 at $17. This is a good example of
a spin-off, once viewed as a low-quality company, that has
appreciated enormously within two years.

Parent	Spin-Off	Spin-Off Date
Interco (ISS)	Florsheim (FLSC)	11/18/94

The firm spun-off its Florsheim Shoes division in a tax free
distribution to shareholders. Shareholders received one share
of Florsheim for every six shares of Interco. Florsheim, a leading manufacturer of men's footwear, targets its products for
the $60-plus segment of the men's nonathletic footwear mar-
ket. Florsheim was abandoned by shareholders after the separation from Interco. Because it was highly leveraged and had
poor cash flow, many thought the company was headed for
Chapter 11. Ironically, Florsheim was a stellar performer in
1996. The stock appreciated a massive 57% and closed the
year at $5 ⅞. Armed with new management and a number of
new products, FLSC's prospects have improved. The appreciation reflects the more optimistic outlook.

Parent	Spin-Off	Spin-Off Date
ITT Corporation (ITT)	Rayonier Inc. (RYN)	3/2/94

ITT spun-off Rayonier (terms: 1:4 ITT), its forest products subsidiary. Rayonier owns or controls approximately 1.5 million
acres of timber resources in the U.S. and New Zealand and
operates three pulp mill and two lumber mills in the U.S.

Parent	Spin-Off	Spin-Off Date
ITT (ITT)	ITT Industries (IIN) & ITT Hartford (HIG)	12/20/95

On June 13, 1995, ITT Corporation announced its plans to
spin-off ITT Hartford and ITT Industries. The restructuring
resulted in three separately traded companies. The transaction, involving sales of $25 billion, was on of the largest of its
kind. The three companies are in the businesses of insurance

services, industrial products, and hospitality, entertainment, and information services. The spin-off ratio was one share of each (ITT, IIN, HIG) for each share of "old" ITT owned. The purpose of the spin-off is to allow ITT Hartford and ITT Industries to independently pursue and separately finance their strategies. ITT's management concluded that the three businesses would be best positioned as independent, publicly owned companies and that the new structure would allow management to focus more intensively on their respective businesses and provide the flexibility for each company to grow in a manner best suited for its industry, with an expected increase in the availability and decrease in the cost of raising capital. In the late 1960s and through the 1970s, ITT acquired more than 250 companies, including Avis Rent-A-Car, Continental Baking Company, Canteen, Rayonier, Sheraton, Hartford Fire Insurance Company, and others.

ITT Industries was formed in September 1995 from the spin-off of ITT Corporation's operating units into three independent, publicly traded companies. ITT Industries has three divisions: Automotive, Defense and Electronics, and Fluid Technology. It sells products in over 100 countries. Cost-cutting programs have been a priority since the company was spun-off from its parent. The stock's performance since its liberation has been uninspiring due to a flattening economy and modest international market growth, but the company's efforts to pare the cost structure should lead to real earnings growth over the next several years. ITT Industries (NYSE: IIN), with over $8 billion in revenues, enjoys either the top or second-best market share in over 75% of its products markets. The revenue is diversified from a global perspective, with over half of its sales generated in North America, 40% from Europe, and 5% from Asia and Latin America. A new, focused, corporate identity and independent stock will motivate management. Growth prospects are stronger, with a more flexible capital structure, and management and shareholder goals are one and the same. Based on IIN's dominant market share, growing opportunities, and possible margin expansion, IIN's stock could gravitate toward $30 or more. The stock was up a modest 2.5% in 1996, closing at $24 ½.

ITT Hartford operates one of the largest multiline insurance companies in the country.

Founded in 1810, ITT Hartford Group Inc. has grown
from a local fire insurance company to a internationally recognized insurance and financial services enterprise. HIG became a public company on December 20, 1995. Prior to the
purchase of ITT Hartford by ITT Corporation in 1970, the
company traded over-the-counter for 80 years. The company
has a large and balanced business mix, reaching markets in
the United States, Canada, Western Europe, Latin America,
and Asia. ITT Hartford offers a broad range of coverages,
including personal auto and homeowners, commercial insurance for small, mid-size, and large accounts, specialty risk
insurance, reinsurance, individual life and annuities, employee benefits, and asset management services. ITT Hartford has compiled a favorable long-term record of growth
and profitability. Operating earnings grew at a 19% compound annual rate from 1990 to 1994 and enjoys a strong
balance sheet. The spin-off should allow HIG to improve
business focus and allocate capital more efficiently. The ITT
Hartford stock began trading on a when-issued basis on December 15, 1995 at $49 ¾. HIG closed 1996 at $67 ½, up 40%.

The "new" ITT refers to itself as the world's largest hotel and gaming company. The new hospitality, entertainment,
and information services giant represents several of the
world's leading brand names and will provide services to
over 100 million people. ITT consists of ITT Sheraton, ITT's
interest in CIGA, Ceasar's World (gaming), a stake in Madi-
son Square Garden, and ITT World Directories(the world's
largest producer of telephone directories). On the gambling
side, the company has announced plans to build new casinos in Nevada and Atlantic City under the Planet Hollywood
name.

Parent	Spin-Off	Spin-Off Date
Kimberly-Clark (KMB)	Schweitzer-Mauduit International (SWM)	12/1/95

On May 9, 1995, Kimberly-Clark announced plans to spin-off
its specialty cigarette paper business in a tax-free distribution.

KMB is a manufacturer of household, personal, and healthcare products. Its consumer products include Kleenex, Huggies diapers and training pants, Kotex, and Scott paper towels. Kimberly, in response to increasingly vocal shareholders, spun-off Schweitzer-Maduit at a ratio of 1 share for every 10 shares of Kimberly-Clark owned. In a increasingly litigious environment, Kimberly wanted to be known as a maker of consumer and healthcare products, not as a supplier to the tobacco industry.

Alpharetta, Georgia–based Schweitzer-Mauduit manufactures paper and tobacco products for the tobacco industry, as well as specialized paper products for use in other applications. SWM produces premium specialty papers and is the world's largest supplier of fine papers to the tobacco industry. The company's products include tipping, plug-wrap papers, and binders for cigars. Its specialized paper products include drinking-straw wrap, lightweight printing papers, tea bags, and coffee and other filter papers. The customer base for the U.S. operations consists of 8 cigarette manufacturers in North America, several cigar manufacturers, and approximately 90 manufacturers in 30 countries outside North America. The company's French operations primarily export to Western Europe and China. Philip Morris accounts for about 35% of sales and is SWM's largest customer. The manufacture of high-quality cigarette papers is complex, and SWM enjoys significant, proprietary advantages, including advanced technology, modern manufacturing capacity, and a solid balance sheet. The strong position of its customers, in combination with long-term supply agreements, permits high-capacity utilization and low-cost raw material sourcing contracts. This allows SWM to achieve high returns of investment and strong cash flow. 1996 was rewarding for SWM shareholders: The stock appreciated 37% and closed at $31 5/8.

Parent	Spin-Off	Spin-Off Date
Kimberly-Clark (KMB)	Midwest Express (MEH)	9/22/95

Midwest Express Holdings was carved-out of Kimberly-Clark. Midwest Express Holdings, Inc. is the holding company for Midwest Express Airlines, a premium-service airlines headquartered in Milwaukee. Operating since 1984, Midwest Express Airlines caters primarily to business travelers and serves 22 cities throughout the United States and Toronto, from its bases of operations in Milwaukee and Omaha, Nebraska. The airline, known for its baked-on-board chocolate chip cookies, roomy leather seats, competitive fares, and all-first-class service, offered stock to the public for the first time on September 22, 1995. The 4.5 million share offering was priced at $18 a share. Prior to the IPO, Midwest Express had been a wholly owned subsidiary of Kimberly-Clark, which started the airline company in 1984. In little more than a decade, the Midwest Express management team transformed the company from an outgrowth of Kimberly-Clark Corporation's internal aviation department to a very successful commercial airlines. The steady growth and profitability culminated in the September 1995 offering, in which Kimberly-Clark reduced its ownership from 100% of Midwest Express to 20%. KMB raised about $92 million in the IPO. Following the offering, MEH had $8 million cash and no debt. KMB sold the remaining 20% interest in the company through a second offering, which was completed in May 1996. The divestiture of MEH was part of a strategy by KMB to concentrate on its core businesses of paper products.

MEH has been flying high since the IPO. Midwest Express stock has outperformed the S&P 500 and S&P Airlines Index. MEH's stock closed 1996 at $36 a share, a 100% increase from the IPO in September 1995. MEH's strategy has worked well. It caters to business travelers in cities that are underserved by other airlines and is the dominant airline at Milwaukee's General Mitchell International Airport. The airline has earned a profit every year since 1987. The rest of the industry lost more than $13 billion from 1990 through 1994. It has a solid reputation among travelers. A Zagat airline survey of frequent airline travelers rated Midwest the best overall U.S. airline.

Parent	Spin-Off	Spin-Off Date
LIN Broadcasting (LINB)	LIN Television Corp. (LNTV)	12/28/94

In January 1995, LIN Broadcasting completed the distribution of the common stock of LIN Television Corp. to shareholders. The transaction enabled LIN TV to pursue more station acquisitions and expand its programming. Lin Television owns and operates eight network-affiliated television stations in the eastern, midwestern, and southern regions of the United States. It also provides programming and marketing services to four TV stations. AT&T's MMM Holdings subsidiary owns a 46% interest in the company.

Parent	Spin-Off	Spin-Off Date
Litton Industries Inc. (LIT)	Western Atlas Inc. (WAI)	3/18/94

Litton Industries, Inc. produces defense electronic systems, computer components, integrated circuits, avionic instruments, and radar warning systems. Litton spun-off its commercial operations, including its oilfield information and industrial automation services (terms: 1:1 LIT). Western Atlas provides oilfield-information, land and marine seismic-survey, well-logging, and reservoir-description services, as well as data interpretation and software equipment. It's industrial-automation business designs integrated manufacturing, automated data-collection, and material-handling and package-handling.

Parent	Spin-Off	Spin-Off Date
Manor Care, Inc. (MNR)	Choice Hotels International (CHH)	11/4/96

On March 7, 1996, Maryland-based Manor Care Inc.'s Board approved the 100% spin-off of the company's lodging business. Shareholders received one share of Choice Hotels International for every share of Manor Care owned. The Internal Revenue Service ruled that the spin-off would be tax-free. Manor Care spun-off Choice Hotels, which owns, manages, or franchises nearly 3,000 hotels. Manor Care will keep its nursing home and healthcare businesses. The spin-off is expected to improve both companies' ability to raise capital to make acquisitions. When the companies merged 15 years ago, revenue from healthcare and lodging were nearly equal, at about $60 million a year. In 1995, Manor Care accounted for 77% of its $1.3 billion in revenues from healthcare and 23% from lodging. Choice Hotels operates under a plethora of brand names: Quality Inns, Comfort Inns, Clarion, Sleep Inns, Rodeway, Econo Lodge, and MainStay Suites. Manor Healthcare develops and manages nursing centers principally for senior citizens (operates 179 nursing and rehab facilities in 28 states). Vitalink provides pharmacy services via 18 sites.

Parent	Spin-Off	Spin-Off Date
Marriott Corp. (HMT)	Marriott International (MAR)	10/11/93

In October 1993, Marriott International was launched as a public company following the division of the Marriott Corporation. Marriott International was spun-off to holders of MHS (terms: 1:1 MHS). Washington, D.C.–based Marriott International, Inc. is the world's leading hospitality company, with approximately 4,600 operating units in 50 states and 28 countries. Major businesses include hotels operated and franchised under the Marriott, Ritz-Carlton, Courtyard, Residence Inn, and Fairfield Inn brands; vacation ownership resorts; food service and facilities management for clients in business, education, and healthcare; senior living communities and services; and food service distribution. The parent was renamed Host Marriott (which later spun-off Host Marriott Services).

Parent	Spin-Off	Spin-Off Date
May Department Store (MA)	Payless ShoeSource (PSS)	5/9/96

May Department Stores spun-off its Payless ShoeSource chain in May 1996. MA shareholders received 0.16 shares of Payless ShoeSource for each share, tax-free. May operates roughly 350 department stores in 30 states through 8 companies: Foley's, Lord & Taylor, Robinsons-May, Hecht's, Kaufman's, Filene's, Famous-Barr, and Meier and Frank. Payless, the largest discount shoe store chain, operates approximately 4,300 self-service stores and 775 Payless Kid's stores. Each store averages 3,000 square feet, and each Payless store carries approximately 11,000 pairs of shoes in over 1,000 different styles with an average retail price of $11.00. Payless is undergoing further restructuring and plans to close 450 stores during 1996. Payless appreciated 45% since the split and closed '96 at $37 ½.

Parent	Spin-Off	Spin-Off Date
Melville Corporation (MES)	Footstar (FTS)	10/16/96

On October 24, 1995, Melville Corporation announced its plan to spin-off Footstar to shareholders. Melville operates specialty-retail stores. It sells prescription drugs and health and beauty aids through stores operating under the CVS Pharmacies name. It sells apparel and accessories in chains of stores operating under the Bob's and Linens 'n' Things names. The company is undergoing a major restructuring, including the spin-off of the footwear businesses and the sale of its KaybeeToys unit for $315 million (previously planned to be spun-off) and the sale of its Wilson's House of Suede and Leather to a management group. In addition, the company plans to distribute to shareholders its interests in Bob's and Linens 'n' Things in two separate spin-offs in mid-1997. The spun-off footwear company consists of Melville's Meldisco, Footaction, and Thom McAnn units, which accounted for $1.82 billion in sales and EBIT of $125 million before special charges in 1995, through approximately 3,300 outlets. In May 1996, Melville announced that it is working to permanently shutter its remaining Thom McAnn's stores.

Parent	Spin-Off	Spin-Off Date
Minnesota Mining and Manufacturing (MMM)	Imation (IMN)	7/16/96

Minnesota Mining and Manufacturing, Inc. spun-off its information-processing businesses in the form of a tax-free distribution to shareholders (ratio 1:10). Management believes that the distribution of Imation will enhance the ability of both 3M and Imation to maximize shareholder values. Each company will be free to pursue its own growth path, without respect to the corporate objectives and policies of the other. This should give Imation greater flexibility to respond to changes in the technology and information-processing markets. Imation started trading July 16, 1996 and opened at 24 ⅛. Imation has over 10,000 products, which are used to capture, store, process, reproduce, and distribute information and images. Its primary products include computer diskettes, data cartridges, computer tapes, rewriteable optical media, CD-ROM replication services, color proofing systems, laser imaging, and X-ray film. The company also has an information processor service group, which supports equipment and engineering and office document support services. Imation generated sales of $2.3 billion in 1995, which would have placed it on the Fortune 500 list of largest manufacturing companies. Over 50% of the firm's sales are generated outside the United States. After the spin-off plan was announced, Imation began a re-engineering process to facilitate sustainable, profitable growth. The changes will include a systematic program to reduce operating costs, trim product portfolios, consolidate plants and facilities, focus on profitable new product solutions, decrease management layers to create a streamlined organization, create new, performance-based compensation structures, outsource noncore competencies, and re-engineer its supply chain with a goal to significantly reduce cycle time.

Parent	Spin-Off	Spin-Off Date
Murphy Oil Corporation (MUR)	Deltic Timber Corporation (DEL)	1/2/97

Eldorado, Arkansas–based Murphy Oil is now focused on petroleum production, after spinning off of its wholly owned farm, timber, and real estate subsidiary Deltic Farm & Timber Co., Inc. (now called Deltic Timber Corporation). Shareholders received 1 share of Deltic Timber for every 3.5 shares of Murphy Oil owned. Management believes the spin-off will increase the ability of Deltic Timber Corporation to achieve and finance its growth, allow the management of each company to focus on its respective core businesses, and enable the financial markets to value each of the companies more accurately. Deltic Timber plans to acquire additional timberlands to supplement its 386,000 acres of land holdings, including 341,000 acres of timberlands.

Parent	Spin-Off	Spin-Off Date
Olin Corporation (OLN)	Primex Technologies (PRMX)	1/7/97

On October 10, 1996, Olin Corporation (NYSE: OLN) approved a plan to spin-off the company's defense and aerospace operations to shareholders to create an independent, publicly traded company. Olin had previously announced that it was considering the action as part of its long-term strategic restructuring. The spin-off was implemented through a special distribution under which 1 share of Premix Technologies' stock was issued for every 10 post-split shares of Olin common stock (or five current shares), resulting in five million shares of Primex common stock outstanding. In response to the news, Olin shares shot $4 ⅜ higher, to close at $88.50 on the New York Stock Exchange.

Headquartered in Norwalk, Connecticut, Olin Corporation is one of the world's leading producers of chemicals, metals, microelectronic materials, and sporting and military ammunition.

Primex Technologies will combine Olin's Ordnance and Aerospace divisions, which together have 2,600 employees and in 1995 had combined revenues of approximately $500 million. PRMX will be headquartered in St. Petersburg, Florida. Olin Management concluded that both Olin and Primex would function better, and appeal more to investors, as independent entities. As a freestanding company, Primex should be better positioned to fund its own business development and concentrate its financial resources wholly on its own operations.

Olin Ordance is a principal producer of conventional military ammunition in the United States and a premier international supplier. Olin Aerospace provides rocket engines, propulsion systems, power supplies, and airborne and space electronics to both government and commercial satellite, aircraft, and missile contractors and to NASA and other government R&D agencies and laboratories.

Parent	Spin-Off	Spin-Off Date
Pacific Telesis (PAC)	AirTouch Communications (ATI)	4/6/94

Airtouch Communications was created as a wholly owned subsidiary of Pacific Telesis so that the parent could spin-off its wireless operations. Pacific Telesis did an IPO of 14% of the subsidiary in December 1993 and spun-off its remaining PacTel shares following the IPO on April 6, 1994 (terms: 1:1 PAC). The spin-off was initiated to separate PAC's wireless communications, which would remove certain regulatory, legal, and financial constraints, allowing PAC to provide long-distance, voice, and data services.

Parent	Spin-Off	Spin-Off Date
Penn Central Corp. (APZ)	General Cable Communication (GENC)	7/2/92

General Cable was spun-off from Penn Central. GENC manufactures wire and cable for the construction, consumer, and telecommunications markets and produces materials-handling machinery and marine equipment.

Parent	Spin-Off	Spin-Off Date
Pittston Company (PZS)	Pittston Minerals Company (PZM)	7/27/93

Pittston split into two companies: Pittston Service Co. (PZS) and Pittston Minerals (PZM). Services retained Pittston's air freight, security, and home-security businesses; Minerals consists of the coal and minerals' business of the Pittston company.

Parent	Spin-Off	Spin-Off Date
Pittston Services Group (PZS, PZM)	Pittston Brinks Group Pittston(PZB) Burlington Group (PZX)	1/22/96

In January 1996, the shareholders of Pittston Services Group voted to divide its shares into two separately traded stocks, Pittston Brinks Group (PZB) and Pittston Burlington Group (PZX), via a tax-free distribution (terms 1:2 Pittston Services Group stock). After the distribution of Pittston Burlington Group shares, Pittston Services changed its name to Pittston Brink's Group, reflecting its remaining businesses. The company provides home security and operates Brink's, the well-known armored care service. Burlington Air Express is a worldwide air freight forwarder focusing on heavy cargo markets.

The purpose of the spin-off is to reclassify the disparate characteristics of the air freight business from the Brink's security services, enabling market valuation of each business based on its own merits.

Parent	Spin-Off	Spin-Off Date
Pittway Corp. (PRY)	Aptar Group, Inc. (ATR)	4/23/93

Aptar Group is a leading manufacturer of dispensing systems for major U.S. and European companies. The firm produces three general product lines: aerosol valves, dispensing closures, and dispensing pumps, sold to the fragrance, personal care, pharmaceutical, food, and household product industries. Pittway Corp. spun-off one share of Aptar Group for every one share of Pittway.

Parent	Spin-Off	Spin-Off Date
Premark International (PMI)	Tupperware (TUP)	5/31/96

Premark International, itself a spin-off from Kraft in 1986, spun-off its Tupperware subsidiary to shareholders via a tax-free divestiture on May 31, 1996. Premark International manufacturers consumer goods, dishwashers, mixers, ovens, weighing equipment, kitchen ranges, and refrigeration equipment sold under brand names such as Hobart, Vulcan, Wolf, Adamati, and Foster. Tupperware manufactures and markets a broad line of high-quality consumer products with particular emphasis on plastic storage products, including food storage containers and stackable, modular, general purpose containers. Tupperware's products are marketed through a direct, independent salesforce of roughly 800,000. Tupperware dominates the U.S. market for such products with a 65% market share. Foreign sales amount to 80% of total revenues.

The purpose of the spin-off was to separate Tupperware's higher margin consumer products business from the slower growth commercial products business. Tupperware's strong cash flow and solid balance sheet can finance growth in the United States and abroad. Recent approval to sell Tupperware products next year in India and China should bode well for future growth, as these two countries account for almost 40% of the world's population. Tupperware stock closed 1996 at $53 ⅝, up 25% since June 1996.

Parent	Spin-Off	Spin-Off Date
Ralston Purina Group (RAL)	Continental Baking (CBG)	8/2/93

Ralston Purina produces pet foods, food additives, chemical products, and consumer products. Ralston Purina Group is the world's largest producer of dry dog and cat foods and dry cell batteries. The company markets its products under the Purina, Dog Chow, Puppy Chow, Cat Chow, Meow Mix, Tender Vittles, Tidy Cat, Eveready, and Energizer brand names. Ralston split into two companies: Ralston Purina Group (RAL) and Continental Baking (terms: 1:5 RAL, which represented 55% of the shareholders' equity value). CBG includes the baking, sale, and delivery of fresh bakery products such as bread, snack cakes, and breakfast pastries.

Parent	Spin-Off	Spin-Off Date
Ralston Purina Group (RAL)	Ralcorp Holdings (RAH)	4/4/94

Ralcorp Holdings, Inc. was incorporated in January 1994 as a subsidiary of the Ralston Group and spun-off from its parent on March 31, 1994, with shareholders receiving one share of the new company for each three Ralston Purina Group shares owned. Ralcorp Holdings processes and distributes consumer food products. These products include cereal, baby food, crackers, cookies, and other snack foods. In 1996 the company agreed to sell its Keystone and Breckenridge ski resorts in Colorado to Vail Resorts for $165 million in cash; Ralcorp will retain a 25% interest in the operations. The sale will allow St. Louis-based Ralcorp to trim its debt load significantly.

On March 29, Ralston Purina announced plans to spinoff its international animal feeds business, which had provided little economic return to shareholders and had previously been up for sale. Pending a favorable (i.e., taxfree) ruling from the IRA, the spin-off is expected to be completed by Spring 1997. The planned spin-off is part of a restructuring that was implemented four years ago by Ralston. Over this time, the company has divested its cereal, baby food, and ski resorts businesses via spin-offs (now held in Ralcorp Holdings, RAH), and it has sold Continental Baking to Interstate Bakeries (Ralston now owns approximately 46% of IBC's common stock). After the spin-off is completed, RAL will be made up of its pet food business, its soy protein business, and its Eveready battery business. Given Ralston's proclivity for spin-offs, I would expect these businesses to be separated at some point.

Parent	Spin-Off	Spin-Off Date
Ruby Tuesday (RI)	Morrison Fresh Cooking (MFC) Morrison Healthcare (MHI)	3/11/96

On September 27, 1995, Ruby Tuesday announced its plan to split the company into three separately traded public firms. Ruby Tuesday operates about 367 casual-dining restaurants under such names as Ruby Tuesdays, Mozzarella's Café, and Tia Tex-Mex. Prior to a March 1996 spin-off, the company was named Morrison Restaurant and owned more than 160 Morrison's Family Dining cafeterias. The purpose of the spinoff was to enable each business to pursue its own growth agenda. No longer will each division have to compete for capital with its former sister divisions or alter strategies in order to benefit the whole organization. The spin-off ratio was one Ruby Tuesday: two RI; one Fresh Cooking: four RI; one Healthcare: three RI.

The separation will enable the management of each company to design corporate policies and strategies that will be based primarily on the characteristics of its own business and to concentrate its financial resources wholly on its own operations. Each company will be in a position to access directly the capital markets and will not compete with one another for allocation of Morrison's financial resources.

The creation of a public market for each of the three businesses will enhance the ability of each company to attract, motivate, and retain qualified executives and key employees by designing programs based on each company's performance. In addition, the newly created securities will facilitate development by enhancing the ability of each company to enter into M&A transactions using its own stock. Management also concluded that the new structure would provide investors and securities analysts a clearer basis on which to analyze the financial performance of the three businesses. The stock of each of the three companies will appeal to investors with differing investment objectives, risk tolerances, and dividend expectations and allow potential investors to direct their investments to their primary areas of interest.

Morrison Fresh Cooking operates the Morrison Family Dining business, 144 cafeteria restaurants and 10 mall foodcourt, quick-service restaurants in 13 states. Based in Atlanta, MFC locates its restaurants in the southeastern and mid-Atlantic regions of the United States in areas convenient to shopping and business developments as well as to residential areas. MFC will be able to move with more speed going forward. The company closed 22 underperforming locations after the spin-off.

MFC's stock has been crushed since the spin-off, falling 47% to end 1996 at $4 ⅝. The stock trades for little more than book value and may be a good speculation.

Morrison Healthcare (MHI) is a company focused on

providing food and nutrition services to healthcare facilities. Until the spin-off, MHI operated as a division of Morrison Restaurants. With approximately 300 accounts, the corporation is one of the leading providers of food and nutrition services to hospitals and healthcare facilities in the nation. MHI is the third largest provider of food and nutrition services for hospitals and healthcare facilities across the United States. MHI is the only pure-plan investment vehicle focused on the growing trend toward outsourcing in healthcare food service (80% of the company's contracts are with hospitals). The company's large, recurring revenue stream provides predictable cash flow with relatively small capital requirements, enabling the company to pay a high dividend. MHI is able to lower costs for its clients through its efficient labor cost controls, greater purchasing power, and superior menu management as compared with self-operated hospital food-service facilities. In addition, the use of branded food-service facilities in the employee and visitor cafeterias typically increases sales, resulting in either higher profits or a reduced food-service subsidy.

MHI has enjoyed a better than 95% retention rate on its account base and the average length of a contract partnership has been 9 to 10 years. This translates into a relatively stable base of operations. Looking beyond 1997, MHI's steady cash flow and substantial operating leverage should enable it to focus on acquisition opportunities and/or pay down debt. MHI's stock closed out 1996 at $14 ¾, down 20%.

Parent	Spin-Off	Spin-Off Date
Ryder Systems (R)	Aviall, Inc.(AVL)	12/15/92

Ryder spun-off its aviation operation Aviall in a tax-free spin-off (terms: 1:4 R). Aviall is the world's largest independent distributor of aviation parts and supplies (92% of revenues). The Dallas–based Aviall also provides inventory information to the aviation industry through Inventory Locator Service, an on-line commercial data provider. The company has struggled since its spin-off from Ryder and has been forced to restructure.

Miami-based Ryder Systems provides highway-transportation services. Through its subsidiaries, the company engages in the leasing and short-term rental of trucks, tractors, and trailers; logistics services; public-transit management; and school bus transportation.

Parent	Spin-Off	Spin-Off Date
Santa Fe Pacific Corp. (SFX)	Santa Fe Pacific Gold Corp. (GLD)	10/1/94

On June 15, 1994, Santa Fe Pacific Crop. completed an IPO representing a 14.6% interest in Santa Fe Pacific Gold at $14 per share. The remaining shares of the common stock (85.4%) were held by its former parent, Santa Fe Pacific Corp., and distributed to its shareholders in a tax-free spin-off on October 1, 1994 (terms: 1:1.7 SFX). Santa Fe Pacific Gold Corporation is engaged in the exploration and development of gold properties and the mining and processing of gold ores. It is one of the largest gold mining firms in North America.

On December 9, Santa Fe Pacific Gold announced that the company agreed to merge with Homestake Mining Corp. in a stock swap worth about $2.3 billion. The swap values Santa Fe at about $17 ½ per share. Should the merger be completed as outlined, the newly formed entity would become the largest North American–based gold company in terms of reserves and the second-largest in terms of production. Santa Fe Pacific Gold shareholders will receive 1.115 new Homestake common shares for each share of GLD. The deal should be completed by April 1997. The combined Homestake/Santa Fe will have annual revenue of $1.1 billion and gold reserves of 39.4 billion ounces. The combined company will focus its exploration in Nevada, Australia, Latin America, and Central America.

Parent	Spin-Off	Spin-Off Date
Samsonite Corp. (SAMC)	Culligan Water Technologies (CUL)	9/13/95

Samsonite separated its business operations into two independent, public companies—Samsonite Corp. and Culligan

Water Technologies. Samsonite distributed Culligan to share-holders via a spin-off (ratio 1:1). Samsonite distributes a full line of luggage, including softside and hardside suitcases, garment/casual bags, business cases, and other travel bags. The restructuring proved to be very successful in creating shareholder value. Culligan Water closed 1996 at $40 ½, up 67% for the year. Samsonite was one of the best-performing stocks in the Russell 2000, shooting up $28 points in 1996 to close $38 ⅜ a share, a return of 284%.

Culligan Water Technologies, Inc. (Northbrook, Illinois) is a leading manufacturer and distributor of water purifica-tion and treatment products for household, commercial, and industrial uses. Culligan is one of the largest and most well-known water treatment companies in North America. Culligan has been active in the water purification and treat-ment industry for 60 years and has one of the strongest fran-chises in the industry. Company name recognition is a direct result of its long-running, high-profile "Hey Culligan Man" marketing campaign, quality products, and its focus on the consumer market. Most of Culligan's sales are directed through the company's extensive network of 1,400 dealers. After being owned as a corporate subsidiary by several dif-ferent companies over 60 years, Culligan was spun-off from Samsonite Corporation (formally Astrum International Corp.) in September 1995 and became a publicly traded entity. Two months later, the company effected a secondary offering and was listed on the NYSE.

Culligan, the market leader in household softeners and the only provider of five-gallon bottled water tanks with a national distribution network, has undergone six major own-ership changes in the last 10 years. Culligan, which intro-duced water softeners to the world in 1936, was sold to the now-defunct Beatrice Cos. in 1978 and since then has passed through the hands of numerous corporate raiders. Though publicly traded, Culligan still is controlled by the financiers who picked up the company from the 1992 bankruptcy of E-II (a holding company controlled by financier Meshulam Riklis). Most of the shares outstanding are closely held. De-spite the December 1995 offering, Apollo Advisors owns 39%,

Carl Icahn owns 22%, and management owns almost 10%. In September 1996, Culligan filed with the SEC for a public offering of 5 million shares held by Steven J. Green and an affiliated entity and entities affiliated with Carl Icahn. The offering will significantly increase the float of Culligan stock, 25% of which was controlled by Green and Icahn prior to the offering.

Although Culligan's stock has appreciated considerably since becoming an independent company, prospects look very favorable for the long term. Culligan is striving to become a "one-stop-shop" in a rapidly consolidating, $25 billion worldwide water industry. Acquisitions will play a large role in Culligan's growth. The company is in the unique position of being able to acquire Culligan dealerships in strategic areas, as it has the right of first refusal on the purchase of many of its franchised dealers. In addition, it will look for complementary acquisitions. Culligan's goal is to grow sales year-to-year at greater than 15%, half internally and half through acquisitions. Recently Culligan entered into a marketing partnership with Health-o-meter, the parent company of Mr. Coffee, for branded, pour-through pitchers carrying the "Water by Culligan" logo. This is a good way for Culligan to leverage its brand into that channel. The company also intends on building its international business, where 40% of CUL's sales are generated and where it enjoys double-digit growth.

The spin-off has been very good to shareholders. Culligan started trading September 13, 1995, at $12.75 a share. Since then the stock has tripled.

Parent	Spin-Off	Spin-Off Date
Sears, Roebuck & Co. (S)	Dean Witter, Discover & Co. (DWD)	7/13/93

A decade ago, Sears, Roebuck & Co. stood as one of America's premier conglomerates, with businesses as diverse as retailing, real estate, consumer credit cards, and insurance. One by one, these units were shed as Sears turned itself into a pure play in retailing. Sears (founded in 1886) is the world's second largest retailer, with more than 800 full-line department stores, more than 600 home-goods stores, and 2,500 automotive stores. June 30, 1995 marked the final chapter of Sears' corporate metamorphosis, as it spun-off the last of its big subsidiaries: Allstate Corp. Though the two companies had been together since 1931, the idea was that each would be better off on its own. This strategy was well received by the market. A year later, the parts of the sum are significantly greater than the previous whole. Sears stock, valued at $17 a share in January 1993, now trades at $54 a share, up 300% in 3 ½ years.

Sears decided to focus on its core business by divesting Coldwell Banker, Dean Witter, Discover & Co., Homart, and Allstate. It was the spin-off of Allstate Corp. that began a new era for Sears, a return to its retailing roots. Gone are insurance, real estate, financial services, and, finally, on-line computer services, with the recent sale of its stake in struggling Prodigy.

Sears' board approved the spin-off of its 80% interest in Dean Witter to Sears common shareholders. Sears' shareholders received .40 shares of Dean Witter for each share of Sears' common stock they held (Dean Witter had completed an IPO on March 1, 1993 at $27 a share). Dean Witter Discover is a financial-services company that provides a range of nationally marketed credit and investment products, with a focus on individuals. The company's two principal businesses are credit-card services and securities. Its credit-services division issues and markets the Discover Card. Dean Witter is a full-service securities business.

Allstate Corp. (founded in 1931) is America's largest publicly held personal-lines (auto, life, and homeowner) insurance company, with more than 20 million customers and 15,000 agents. The company was spun-off in June 1993 with the issuance of 439 million shares at $27 each in the then largest initial public offering in the history of the NYSE (since surpassed by the Lucent Technologies IPO). Sears spun-off the remaining 80% of Allstate Insurance in June 1995. The stock essentially doubled its 1993 levels and is currently trading at record highs.

Parent	Spin-Off	Spin-Off Date
Signet Banking Corporation (SBK)	Capital One Financial Corp. (COF)	3/2/95

Signet Banking Corporation is a multibank holding company with about 250 branches in Virginia, Maryland, and Washington, D.C. Signet Bank's services include credit cards, student loans, trusts, brokerage, mortgage banking, and insurance. The company's capital-markets division trades U.S. and foreign securities, manages individuals portfolios, and provides venture-capital funding for new businesses.

On November 15, 1994, Signet IPO'd 11.5% of Capital One Corp., its bank-card issuing subsidiary, at $16 per share. It spun-off the remaining 88.5% interest to shareholders of Signet on March 1, 1995. Capital One is one of the oldest operating bank-card issuers in the country. Currently, Capital One Financial is one of the 10 largest issuers of Visa and Mastercard credit cards in the United States, based on its $10.4 billion in outstanding loans. COF has approximately 6 million credit-card accounts. The firm employs an information system that sorts customers' payment histories and bank-card usage to define the optimal bank-card offer. This system is cited by management as a critical factor in their explosive growth over the last several years. The spin-off has indeed unlocked value, as COF currently trades in the low 30s per share.

Parent	Spin-Off	Spin-Off Date
Sprint Corp. (FON)	360 Communications (XO)	3/8/96

Sprint Corp. completed a tax-free spin-off of its cellular unit, 360 Communications, to shareholders on March 7, 1996. Sprint is a long-distance and local telephone carrier. Its local operating companies provide telecommunication services to more than 8 million customers and publish 325 directories in 20 states. Chicago-based 360 Communications provides wireless voice and data service to more than 1.5 million customers in nearly 100 markets across 14 states. 360 Communications operates cellular systems in 87 metropolitan and rural service areas in 14 states and has ownership interests in 52 other markets, representing more than 20 million people.

Holders of Sprint common stock as of February 27, 1996 received one share of 360 for every three shares Sprint. 360 is the second largest pure play after Airtouch Communications (also a spin-off). The company started trading on the New York Stock Exchange on March 8, 1996, at $23 ½ a share, implying an equity market cap of $2.7 billion. The company closed 1996 at $23 ¼.

360 Communications was established in June 1984. Initially the company, then known as Centel Cellular, acquired cellular control in 12 markets. In 1988 the company more than doubled its size by acquiring United TeleSpectrum from Sprint. Five years later, Centel merged with Sprint and changed its name to Sprint Cellular. In July 1995, Sprint announced plans to spin-off its cellular division. The company has grown at a rate of more than 50 percent a year since 1992.

The purpose of the spin-off was to overcome the regulatory hurdle for developing the company's PCS joint venture with Comcast, Cox, and Telecommunications. In order to pursue the PCS opportunity, Sprint was required to divest its cellular franchises in Philadelphia, Dallas–Fort Worth, Detroit, and Des Moines/Quad Cities. Sprint chose to spin-off its entire cellular business as the best alternative for its shareholders.

Parent	Spin-Off	Spin-Off Date
Sterling Software (SSW)	Sterling Commerce (SE)	10/7/96

The company completed a partial IPO of 13.8 million shares of Sterling Commerce at $24 per share on March 8, 1996. Sterling Commerce develops and provides electronic-commerce software products and network services. Sterling Software (SSW) spun-off the remaining shares of Sterling Commerce (SE) to shareholders on the basis of 1.59260 shares of Sterling Commerce stock for every share of Sterling Software held. The dividend was paid pro rata to the holders of record of September 30, 1996. The purpose of the spin-off was to increase the unit's financial flexibility and highlight its position in the fast-growing electronic commerce business.

Sterling Software's products and services include electronic data-interchange software, data-communication software, and electronic-payments software for financial institutions. Dallas-based SSW has a worldwide installed base of more than 20,000 customer sites and has 2,600 employees in 70 offices worldwide. The spin-off, Sterling Commerce (SE), is a leading, global provider of electronic software products and network services that enable companies to engage in business-to-business electronic communications and transactions, including electronic mail, electronic bulletin boards, electronic funds transfers, and electronic-catalog services. Sterling Commerce has been providing electronic commerce solutions for over 20 years and has nearly 20,000 customer sites worldwide and more than 1,100 employees.

Sterling Commerce is poised to produce sustainable annual earnings growth of 30% for the next three years. With a growing core business, the company is generating strong earnings momentum and cash flow. Guided by an experienced management team, Sterling Commerce is well positioned to leverage its dominant competitive position and take advantage of rapidly expanding market opportunities. Sterling Software returned 40% to its shareholders in 1996. Sterling Commerce closed at $35 ¼, up 22% on the year.

Parent	Spin-Off	Spin-Off Date
Tele-Communications (TCOMA)	TCI Satellite Entertainment (TSATA)	12/5/96

Tele-Communications (TCI) operates the nation's largest cable-television system and provides cable-programming services. On June 19, 1996, it announced plans to spin-off its satellite broadcast operation. The satellite unit has a 21% interest in Primestar Partners, LP, which relays television programs to about 1.5 million subscribers who own 36-inch satellite dishes. The partnership is used as a marketing company to compete against other direct-broadcast satellite companies such as DirecTV, which is owned by Hughes

Communications. The unit has a ground distribution network which covers about 40% of the potential marketplace for direct-broadcast satellite within the country. The spin-off was approved to create a currency for the satellite unit.

The TCI Satellite Entertainment shares were distributed December 5, 1996 to Tele-Communications shareholders. Holders of record (record date established as November 12, 1996) of TCI Group common stock received 1 share of Series A common stock of TCI Satellite Entertainment for each 10 shares of Series A TCI Group common stock and 1 share of Series B common stock of TCI Satellite Entertainment for each 10 shares of Series B common stock.

Parent	Spin-Off	Spin-Off Date
Tenneco (TEN)	Newport News Shipbuilding (NNS)	12/12/96

In a continuing quest to unlock and maximize shareholder value, Tenneco spun-off the Newport News Shipbuilding unit and sold the Tenneco Energy division to El Paso Energy, leaving the company with its Evanston, Illinois–based Tenneco Packaging and Deerfield, Illinois–based Tenneco Automotive units. The restructuring takes Tenneco out of the energy business it first entered in 1943 and makes Newport News Shipbuilding an independent company. The "new" Tenneco will attempt to double revenue and triple earnings within five years at the packaging and automotive units. The packaging unit, which makes Hefty and Baggies brand plastic bags, is the fourth-largest packaging operation in North America, and Tenneco Automotive makes one of every four shock absorbers and mufflers sold worldwide. Through the first nine months of 1996, the units generated $4.9 billion in sales and $586 million in operating income. Under terms of the restructuring, Tenneco shareholders received 1 share of Tenneco stock and 1 share of Newport News Shipbuilding for every 5 shares of Tenneco stock held, and 1 share of El Paso Energy for roughly 10 shares of Tenneco.

Under CEO Dana Mead's leadership, Tenneco has undergone a transformation from an unwieldy conglomerate to a company focused on a handful of core businesses. Each of these businesses is an industry leader and expected to be highly profitable on a stand-alone basis. The corporate demerger of Tenneco into separate operating companies has the potential to unleash value for shareholders. Some analysts feel the parts are worth $75.

Newport News Shipbuilding

Newport News Shipbuilding is one of the most technologically advanced industrial complexes in the world. Located in Newport News, Virginia, it is staffed and equipped to design, build, overhaul, and repair a full range of nuclear-powered and conventional ships for both defense and commercial applications. The company also provides various industries with engineering and computer-based services and industrial products. While Newport News Shipbuilding cannot be viewed as a growth story, the shipyard *is* a strong generator of free cash flow. It is the only shipyard in the world that is capable of building, overhauling, and refueling both nuclear aircraft carriers and nuclear submarines. The company is striving to diversify its revenue mix, currently 90% navy and 10% commercial, to 65% navy and 35% commercial by 1999. The stock finished 1996 at $15 a share.

Automotive

Tenneco Automotive is a global manufacturer and marketer of automotive parts for both OEM and replacement markets. Tenneco Automotive consists primarily of Monroe (shocks and struts) and Walker (exhaust systems). The company is first in aftermarket share and either first or second in original-equipment market share in North America, Europe, and Australia. The company has excellent growth prospects as a result of accelerated global expansion, acquisitions, and new products and processes.

Packaging

Packaging Corporation of America (PCA) is a leading diversified-packaging company. It is America's largest supplier and

producer of food containers made from clear plastic, aluminum foil, and molded fiber. It is also the country's largest
supplier of corrugated containers and is a major manufacturer of folding cartons, recycled paperboard, and
containerboard.

Parent	Spin-Off	Spin-Off Date
Travelers Group (TRV)	Transport Holdings (TLIC)	10/2/95

Travelers Group provides insurance, managed healthcare,
and investment services.

Transport Holdings, Inc. was spun-off as a special dividend to stockholders of Travelers Group Inc. on September
29, 1995. The record date for the distribution was September
11, 1995. Shareholders received 1 share of Transport Holdings for every 200 shares of Travelers Group common stock.
The first trade was on October 2, at $36 a share, and the stock
traded around $40 per share through the end of the year.
Transport Holdings Inc. is an insurance holding company
whose principal subsidiary, Transport Life Insurance Company, is a Texas life insurance company specializing in supple-
mental life and health insurance coverages. TLIC sells a
variety of cancer, heart, and accident policies.

On September 26, 1996, Conseco Inc. and Transport
Holdings Inc. signed a merger agreement under which
Conseco would acquire Transport for $70 a share in Conseco
stock. The total value of the deal was approximately $311
million, including $228 million to purchase 3.2 million com-
mon shares of Transport and $83 million to retire bank debt
and preferred stock. On December 23, 1996, the merger was
completed. Each outstanding share of Transport common
stock was converted into the right to receive 1.4 shares of
common stock of Conseco (CNC), a financial services company. This is a another example of a spin-off that gets bought
out shortly after being divested.

Parent	Spin-Off	Spin-Off Date
Union Carbide Corp. (UK)	Praxair (PX)	7/6/92

Praxair is the largest supplier of industrial gases in the Western Hemisphere and the third largest worldwide. The gases are used in the metal-fabrication, primary-metals, chemicals, electronics, oil & gas, food-processing, and pulp & paper industries. Union Carbide spun-off the company on a one-for-one basis in July 1992. UK is a producer of ethylene glycol, polyethylene, solvents, coatings, and specialty chemicals.

Parent	Spin-Off	Spin-Off Date
Union Pacific (UNP)	Union Pacific Resources (UPR)	10/16/96

On October 16, 1996, Union Pacific Corporation completed the pro-rata, tax-free distribution to its shareholders of all its remaining shares of common stock of Union Pacific Resources Group Inc. (UPR). UPR was spun-off on the basis of .846946 shares of Resources' common stock for each Union Pacific common share held on the record date of September 26, 1996. Resources, now fully independent, is one of the nation's most successful natural gas and oil companies. Headquartered in Fort Worth, Texas, Resources is involved in the exploration for and the development and production of natural gas, natural gas liquids, and crude oil. It is one of the largest independent energy companies in North America. The company also engages in hard mineral mining through nonoperated joint ventures and has royalty interests in several coal and trona mines. Trona is mined and processed into natural soda ash. Soda ash is used to make glass, detergents, baking soda, and industrial chemicals.

The spin-off was completed in a two-step process. Union Pacific Corporation spun-off 17 percent of Union Pacific Resources in an initial public offering at $21 per share, completed in October 1995. The remaining 83% ownership interest was distributed pro rata to its shareholders as a dividend in October 1996. UPR was added to the Standard & Poor's 500 index.

Union Pacific (UNP) primarily operates railroads in the United States and Canada. Its Union Pacific Railroad subsidiary owns about 17,500 miles of track. The company agreed to acquire Southern Pacific Rail in 1995.

Parent	Spin-Off	Spin-Off Date
U.S. Long Distance (USLD)	Billing Information Concepts (BILL)	8/5/96

On May 14, 1996, the Board of Directors of U.S. Long Distance announced their intent to distribute one share of Billing Information Concepts for each share of U.S. Long Distance held. The spin-off was approved to eliminate conflicts between USLD and other long-distance providers that use the services of the billing unit. San Antonio, Texas–based U.S. Long Distance is a fully integrated, long-distance telecommunications company providing a full range of direct-dial (1+) long-distance services to its customer base of small- to medium-size businesses and residents in the Southwest, West, and Pacific Northwest. The firm also provides national operator services (0+) to multiphone facilities such as hotels, resorts, hospitals, and universities, as well as to the private owners of public pay phones. The company spun-off its billing and collection services unit, Billing Information Concepts, issuing one share of BILL for each share of USLD owned as of the close of business on July 29, 1996. The stock began trading on August 5, 1996, and opened at $21 ½. The stock closed out 1996 at $28 ¾, up 34% in only five months of trading.

Billing Information Concepts Corp. is a third-party billing clearinghouse for the telecommunications industry. BILL processes telephone-call records for its customers (primarily long-distance telephone companies and operator service providers) and delivers them to local telephone companies, which include the call records in their monthly bills. When the end-user pays, the local telephone companies remit money back to BILL which, in turn, remits payment to its customers. BILL is well positioned to capitalize on potentially large billing opportunities from telecom deregulation. The company is currently negotiating with a number of regional Bell telephone companies to provide them with in-region and out-of-region long-distance billing services. BILL is the dominant third-party telecommunication billing clearinghouse, with about 80% market share in outsourced long-distance billing and 40% market share in outsourced operator-service billing. Billing Information Concepts has demonstrated strong growth over the last several years, with a five-year compounded annual revenue growth rate of 61%. Operating margins are in the 22 to 24% range. BILL was well received by the investment community, trading in the 30s within several months.

Parent	Spin-Off	Spin-Off Date
Valspar Inc. (VAL)	McWhorter Tech, Inc. (MWT)	5/2/94

Founded 188 years ago as the first manufacturer of spar varnish in America, Valspar has grown dramatically in the past 10 years, largely by acquisitions, to become a premier domestic manufacturer of paints and coatings. Valspar is pushing aggressively into Europe and Asia after decades of focusing only on the US market. April 1994, Valspar spun-off its McWhorter division to shareholders in a tax-free distribution. Valspar reached an agreement with the Federal Trade Commission allowing McWhorter to acquire the Resin Products Division of Cargill, Inc. Under the agreement with the FTC, Valspar was required to spin-off the McWhorter Technology unit (terms: 1:2 VAL). McWhorter Technologies is a specialty chemical company which develops, manufactures, and markets a broad range of resin products and technologies for the coatings and fiberglass industries. In addition to its proprietary products, McWhorter also toll manufactures customers' technologies to their specifications. In 1995, the company earned $11.1 million on sales of $311.4 million. The company has managed to achieve a successful record during the past ten years, including an average annual return on equity (ROE) of 21.6% and a net income compound annual growth rate (CAGR) of 16.1%.

Parent	Spin-Off	Spin-Off Date
W.R. Grace (GRA)	National Medical Care	9/29/96

September 29, 1996, W.R. Grace & Co. completed the spin-off to its common shareholders of a new company comprising its packaging and specialty chemicals businesses, and the

combination of its former healthcare subsidiary, National
Medical Care, Inc., with the dialysis business of Frensenius
AG. Prior to the deal, Grace received $2.3 billion from Na-
tional Medical Care, improving GRA's debt to capital ratio
significantly. Grace common shareholders received 44.8 percent of the newly created healthcare company, named
Frensenius Medical Care (the world's largest fully integrated
renal care company) and 100% of the new W.R. Grace & Co.
For each Grace common share outstanding at the close of
business on September 27, 1996, Grace shareholders received
one share of new Grace stock, one share of a new class of
preferred stock, and 1.049099 American depository shares,
each representing a third of an ordinary share of Frensenius
Medical Care (NYSE: FMS). New Grace common shares
started trading on a when-issued basis on September 17, 1996,
and on a regular way basis on October 1, 1996.

New W.R. Grace produces specialty chemicals and food
service packaging products. Its core chemical lines include
products used in petroleum, construction, and water-treat-
ment industries. Since Grace completed the spin-off of its
kidney-dialysis unit, National Medical Care, it has sold three
other noncore businesses.

Parent	Spin-Off	Spin-Off Date
WMS Industries (WMS)	Midway Games (MWY)	10/29/96

When WMS Industries announced a major restructuring, the
company approved a plan to separate into three distinct operations as follows: a spin-off of 100% of WMS's Puerto Rico–
based hotel, casino, and management business to the
company's stockholders; an initial public offering of approximately 15% of the company's coin-operated video-arcade and
home video-game business Midway (MWY) by October 1996;
and the downsizing of the company's pinball machine business.

WMS produces coin-operated amusement games. These
games include pinball, video, shuffle-alley, video-lottery terminals, and electronic games. Its games are sold under the

Williams, Bally, Midway, and Tradewest brand names. The company acquired Atari Games in 1996.

Midway Games was a wholly owned subsidiary of WMS Industries Inc. WMS owns 86.8% of the outstanding shares of common. Midway is a designer, publisher, and marketer of interactive entertainment software played in both the coin-operated and home markets. Since the late 1970s, Midway has released many of the industry's leading games including Mortal Combat, NBA JAM, Pacman, and Space Invaders, and other games through its recently acquired Atari Games subsidiary. Midway's revenue increased to $245.4 million in fiscal 1996, from $180.5 million in fiscal 1995.

WMS Industries is an excellent example of how companies involved in spin-offs can be priced inefficiently. On January 16, 1997, you could buy WMS stock for $23 a share. This would seem to be a true bargain trading at a large discount to the implied value of its holdings. Why? Because the casino operator and maker of gambling and pinball machines carved out Midway games in October in an initial public offering. But WMS still owns 86.8% of Midway, or about 33 million shares outstanding. That means that each share of WMS effectively owns 1.38 shares of Midway. Midway shares closed at $20 ¼ on January 16, meaning each share of WMS owned $27.95 worth of Midway Stock. But WMS stock closed at only $23 ⅛. Assuming that all of WMSs other assets are worth nothing, it is still trading at a 18% discount to the implied value of it's Midway holdings. This is a very dramatic discount and illustrates that bargains sometimes are available in spin-off situations.

So, how do you take advantage of this discrepancy in pricing? Arbitrageurs would short the Midway stock and buy the WMS shares and wait for the market to correct itself. Why has this not happened? Probably because the float in Midway is too small (only 5 million shares in public hands). This would make it difficult to borrow the Midway shares to short sell. So how will an investor be able to realize the value of Midway? Buy WMS stock and hope that they are smart enough to spin-off the Midway stake to shareholders to get the value recognized.

Besides the $28 interest in Midway, WMS has roughly $3 a share of value in its casinos in Puerto Rico and perhaps $1.50 a share of cash net of debt. In addition, WMS has businesses making slot, video lottery and pinball machines. This apparent bargain has enticed Sumner Redstone, CEO of Viacom, to buy nearly 1 million shares of WMS in January at around $20 a share, raising his stake to 6.9 million shares, or 29% of the outstanding stock.

Parent	Spin-Off	Spin-Off Date
Westmark Int'l (WGHI)	Spacelabs Medical Inc. (SLMD)	6/29/92

Westmark was split into two separate companies: Spacelabs Medical (SLMD) and Advanced Technology Laboratories (ATLI). On June 29, Westmark spun-off Spacelabs Medical to its shareholders, distributing one share of SpaceLabs for each share of Westmark. Redmond, Washington–based SpaceLabs Medical manufactures patient-monitoring and clinical-information systems used in health-care applications. The company's patient-monitoring systems consist of monitors and modules that measure and display a patient's vital signs, including blood pressure, temperature, respiration, and blood-oxygen saturation. Its clinical-information systems store a record of a patient's historical and current condition in a computer, allowing charts to be created using these data.

Parent	Spin-Off	Spin-Off Date
Wilcox & Gibbs, Inc. (WG)	Worldtex Inc. (WTX)	12/15/92

In April 1992, Wilcox and Gibbs announced a plan to enhance shareholder value. As part of the plan, Wilcox and Gibbs completed the spin-off of its covered yarn manufacturing business to shareholders on a tax-free basis (terms: 1:1 WG). The company is the largest manufacturer of covered yarn in the world, used principally in the manufacture of apparel and women's hosiery. Worldtex's principal product is nylon-covered spandex, used in the manufacture of various men's women's, and children's apparel.

PART **THREE**

THE FUTURE

CHAPTER 8.

Pending Spin-Offs

AMERICAN BRANDS
Announced 10/8/96

American Brands (NYSE: AMB) announced plans to spin-off its UK-based Gallaher tobacco business in a transaction that will be tax-free to U.S. shareholders and, when the transaction is consummated, will change the name of American Brands to Fortune Brands.

After the completion of the transaction, American Brands shareholders will own shares in two publicly traded companies: Gallaher—the number 1 tobacco company in the United Kingdom; and Fortune Brands, a $4.6 billion company that will consist of American Brands' nontobacco consumer brands.

U.S. holders of record of AMB stock at the time of the spin-off will receive their Gallaher shares in the form of American Depository Receipts (ADRs). It is expected that Gallaher ADRs will trade on the New York Stock Exchange and Gallaher ordinary shares on the London Stock Exchange.

Fortune Brands: A Major Consumer Products Company

The nontobacco operations of American Brands, which will become Fortune Brands, had sales of $4.6 billion for the 12 months ended June 1996. Eleven brands each achieved sales exceeding $100 million: Titleist, Jim Beam, Master Lock, Day-Timer, ACCO, Moen, Cobra, Foot-Joy, DeKuyper, Wilson Jones, and Aristokraft. Fortune Brands has powerful brands in each of the categories in which it competes—hardware, distilled spirits, office products, and golf. Fortune Brands is number one or number two in each of these categories. After the separation, management wishes to grow long-term EPS in the 13 to 15% range. That is considerably greater than the 10% goal established for American Brands.

Gallaher

Gallaher has sales of over $6.5 billion and is the UK tobacco market leader. It is the number one company in the Republic of Ireland and has a growing presence in continental Europe and the former Soviet Union. Its major brands include Benson and Hedges, Silk Cut, Hamlet, Condor, and Old Holborn.

AMERICAN BRANDS
1700 E. Putnum Ave.
Old Greenwich, CT 06870
Contact: D.A. Conforti, 203-698-5132

ASHLAND
Announced 1/30/97

Ashland announced it will carve-out 20% of Ashland Exploration in an IPO in the spring or summer of 1997. Ashland intends to follow the IPO with a tax-free spin-off of the rest of the company to shareholders by the end of '97. Ashland Exploration is a domestic and international producer of natural gas and crude oil. The unit had total proven reserves of 577 billion cubic feet of natural gas and 21.5 million barrels of crude oil as of September 30, 1996. The spin-off will free capital investment for areas expected to yield greater returns. The unit accounted for 10 percent of Ashland Inc.'s revenues in fiscal 1996 ended September 30. The unit is well positioned to grow its core operations in the Appalachian Basin, the Gulf of Mexico, and Nigeria.

Ashland Inc.'s primary businesses are petroleum refining and marketing, along with chemicals and energy. They
do not have a major presence in exploration. The exploration
unit required significant capital. Ashland operates energy and
construction businesses, holds interests in approximately
4,350 oil and natural gas wells in the United States and Nigeria, and holds net reserves of almost 16 million barrels of oil
and 427 billion cubic feet of gas. The company owns three
refineries, 700 SuperAmerica and Rich Oil gas stations, and
365 Valvoline quick-oil-change centers, and produces lubricants and automotive fluids under the Valvoline and Pyroil
names. Ashland also has coal-mining interests.

ASHLAND INC.
PO Box 391
Ashland, Kentucky 41114
Contact: Stan Lampe 606-329-3333

C-TEC
Announced 2/13/97

C-TEC Corp. (CTEX, CTEXB), a telecommunications and
cable television company, announced it will separate into
three publicly held companies by spinning off two units to
its shareholders. C-TEC, based in Princeton, New Jersey, said
it will separate into RCN Corp., C-TEC Corp., and C-TEC
Cable Systems of Michigan Inc., and spin-off the stock of RCN
(a start-up that provides a variety of residential telecommunications services on the East Coast) and C-Tec Cable Systems (a Michigan cable company). The stock closed at $27 ⅝,
up a dollar.

C-TEC Corp. is a holding company with wholly owned
subsidiaries that are involved in various aspects of the communication industry and are organized into four principal
groups: Telephone, cable television, communications services,
and long distance. The company provides local telephone
service to a 5,000-square-mile service territory in Pennsylvania and long-distance service in the state. Its cable division
operates cable-television systems in New York, New Jersey,

Michigan, and Delaware, serving 335,000 customers. C-TEC's communication services include telephone-system integration and operation and management of telecommunication facilities for corporate clients, hospitals, and universities in the northeastern United States. All the businesses combined accounted for $367.3 million in revenue in 1996.

C-TEC joins the growing list of companies that have recently moved to spin-off units or split into separate, publicly traded companies to boost shareholder value. Under the plan, C-TEC's operations will be separated into three independent companies:

■ **RCN Corporation (RCN)** will consist of RCN Telecom Services, which provides competitive video and telecommunications services in Boston and New York, the company's New York, New Jersey, and Pennsylvania cable television operations, and its investment in Megacable S.A. de C.V., Mexico's largest cable MSO. The RCN Telecom Services Unit (which provides residential telecommunications services) generated cash flow of $12.5 million on revenue of $106 million in 1996.

■ **C-TEC Corporation**, which will be renamed CTCo and will consist of the company's local telephone operations (comprised of the telephone service in rural Pennsylvania) and related engineering business. The company currently serves 240,000 access lines in rural Pennsylvania. For the year ended 1996, the company posted an 8% increase in revenues to $139 million and a 7% increase in EBITDA to $80.6 million. Increased customer demand for connections to the Internet, combined with growth in access minutes, mainly accounted for the substantial gains.

■ **C-TEC Cable Systems of Michigan, Inc.,** which will consist of the company's classic cable television operations in Michigan, including its 62% interest in Mercom, Inc. (NASDAQ: MEEO). The Michigan cable unit generated cash flow of $35 million on revenue of about $75 million last year, with 200,000 subscribers.

Management believes that the restructuring will help the financial market to better understand and evaluate the company's various businesses and help RCN raise capital on more efficient terms. Chairman David C. McCourt, feels the spin-off is the best way to close the gap between the value of the business and value currently perceived by the investment market. It is anticipated that the spin-offs will occur by year-end.

C-TEC
105 Carnegie Center
Princeton, NJ 08540
Contact: Valerie Haertel 609-734-3816

CULBRO
Announced 12/24/96

Culbro (NYSE: CBO) produces tobacco and consumer products, nursery plants, and packaging products. It also manages commercial and residential real estate. The firm's consumer products segment manufactures cigars, cigarettes, food-service products, health and beauty aids, candy, paper, and general merchandise.

Culbro Corp. said it agreed to buy Villazon & Co., a Tampa, Florida, cigar maker, and its Honduran affiliate in a transaction valued at $89 million. Villazon makes such leading, premium Honduran cigars as Punch, Hoyo de Monterrey, and Hoyo de Monterrey Excalibur. The acquisition will comprise General cigar factories in Honduras, where Villazon makes handmade cigars, and Tampa, where the company makes machine-made cigars. The company also said it expects to offer shares of its General Cigar Holdings Inc. unit to the public in February as part of a restructuring. Investors applauded Culbro Corp.'s plan to publicly sell shares of its General Cigar unit, pushing the stock up to $60 a share. If the cigar unit offering is successful, Culbro said it also may distribute to its shareholders shares of its nontobacco businesses. General Cigar plans to offer six million shares in a range of $14 to $16 each, according to documents filed with the Securities and Exchange Commission. General Cigar posted 1996 operating profit of $32 million on sales of $196.7 million, after giving effect to an acquisition. Culbro will retain 97% of the voting power of the company by giving the Class A common stock limited voting power. Each Class A share will be worth only one vote, while each share of Class B stock, to be held by Culbro, will have 10 votes. The shares will trade on the NYSE under the proposed symbol MPP.

The General Cigar Holdings unit makes Macanudo, the best-selling premium cigar sold in the United States, along with Partagas and other premium brands. These hand made brands are produced in the company's Jamaican and Dominican Republic cigar factories. General also makes machine-made cigars, such as Garcia y Vega in Alabama.

Culbro is a far different company today than it was in 1993. Culbro removed Eli Witt Co., a cigarette and general merchandise distributor, from its balance sheet by cutting its stake in the company from 85 to 50.1% in April 1994. In June 1996, Culbro signed a letter of intent to sell its $51 million labeling systems and packaging machinery business. Culbro in now a $220 million dollar business that is increasingly focused on the cigar business. This enhanced the value of the stock; Wall Street bid up cigar companies as demand far outstripped supply for cigars in recent years as Americans have embraced cigar smoking. Culbro languished between $13 and $18 in 1994; today, the stock trades at nearly $70, about 400 percent above its low of two years ago, and had traded as high as $76 ¾ in 1996. The cigar boom, which began in late 1992 and exploded in 1995 and 1996, has continued to draw interest from investors.

CULBRO CORPORATION
387 Park Avenue South
New York, NY 10016
212-561-8700

THE DIANA CORPORATION
Announced: 11/21/96

The Diana Corporation (NYSE: DNA) announced its plan to separate the company into two new, publicly traded entities: the original company, which will be renamed Sattel Communications, Inc., and a newly formed company, NEWCO. The plan is to retain Sattel Communications, a provider of central office telephony and Internet switching equipment, for telecommunications carriers and to trade on the NYSE after the restructuring.

The restructuring also calls for the Atlanta Provision Company (APC), C&L Communications, Inc. (C&L), and Valley Communications, Inc. (Valley) to be grouped together into NEWCO, which is expected to trade on the NASDAQ. NEWCO will distribute telecommunications equipment, install and service voice and data networks, and distribute meat and seafood. NEWCO shares will be a dividend to holders of record of Diana common stock. *The distribution of the new shares will constitute a taxable distribution to stockholders.* Management believes that the separation will enable the marketplace to value the business as an independent company, which will enhance its ability to attract capital.

Sattel

Sattel Communications, headquartered in Calabasas, California, designs, develops, engineers, and markets scalable, public network-based central office telephony and Internet switching systems for emerging and traditional telecommunications carriers and Internet service providers worldwide. Sattel's DSS switching systems provide cost-effective, versatile access to voice, data, and video services on the public telephone network and the Internet.

NEWCO

After the distribution, NEWCO, through its subsidiaries, will continue as a telecommunications equipment distributor, voice, and data network installation and service provider, and wholesale distributor of meat and seafood.

THE DIANA CORPORATION
8200 W. Brown Deer Road
Milwaukee, WI 53223
414-355-0037

ELCO INTERNATIONAL
Announced 10/12/96

Elco International (ELCO) announced on October 12 that it was considering taking public one of its two units, Elcom Systems Inc. The technology subsidiary develops and licenses the company's electronic commerce software system. In order to support the possible offering, the company said it would continue to invest higher-than-anticipated amounts in additional sales and in technical and support staffing of Elcom Systems. The stock trades at $8 a share. A partial public offering would help the real worth of the unit, boosting the overall value of parent.

Elcom's other unit, Catalink Direct, which produced revenues last year of $123 million, resells computer equipment using its proprietary Personal Electronic Catalog & Ordering System (PECOS). This is the Elcom System that is to be spun-off. Some feel that Elcom Systems is worth $4 or $5 a share alone. The Catalink unit is obscuring the true value of Elcom's proprietary technology. The company is currently developing a PECOS system that will communicate over the Internet.

Founded in 1992, Elcom International, Inc. develops and markets software systems that enable companies to conduct electronic commerce on private telephone systems and via the Internet. Catalink Direct uses this electronic commerce technology to market and sell personal computer products to business and corporate customers. Catalink began operations in 1993 and has revenues in excess of $580 million, a substantial portion which is conducted via PECOS.

The company is positioned and staffed to benefit from what is expected to be rapid growth in electronic commerce in coming years. ELCO, which came public in mid-December 1995 at $11, has slid to $8 as large corporations have become a more important component of the company's revenue mix, aiding sales but placing pressure on gross margin. If the company succeeds in broadening the application of its PECOS technology, the company is capable of 30% plus earnings growth. The company raised $41 million in its IPO in December 1995. The company at the end of the June quarter had $24 million in cash and no long-term debt.

ELCOM INTERNATIONAL
10 Oceana Way
Norwood, MA 02062
Contact: Eric Poley 617-440-3333

EQUIFAX
Announced: 12/9/96

Atlanta, Georgia–based Equifax announced plans to split into two independent companies, separating its financial and insurance services operations. This will be accomplished through a spin-off of the Insurance Services Group, giving Equifax stockholders direct ownership of the group. The spin-off is designed as a tax-free dividend to shareholders.

Equifax provides information-based administrative services to businesses and governments throughout the United States and in nine foreign countries. The company's Equifax Credit Information and its Credit Northwest subsidiaries provide information and administration services for consumer and commercial credit-report services. Equifax provides information for insurance-underwriting purposes.

The split is being pursued because the corporation's two business groups have diverged in their products, customers, and strategies, management said. Equifax sees the split as a opportunity to establish more focused, swifter companies. The 97-year-old company has revenues of $1.7 billion and has posted 19 consecutive quarters of record earnings. Until the spin-off takes place, the management and structure of Equifax will remain unchanged. Once the spin-off is completed, David McGlaughlin will become vice chairman and CEO of Equifax. C.C. Rogers Jr. will continue to serve as chairman of the Equifax.

Once finalized, current shares will reflect a new Equifax represented by the Financial Services Group, which already is a world leader in the fast-growing financial information markets. With $1.2 billion in annual revenue and sales in 40 countries, the new Equifax is known for credit and commercial information, card processing, check authorization, analytics and consulting, econometric forecasting, and financial software.

The insurance spin-off, with $559 million in annual revenue and more than 4,500 employees, will continue to specialize in providing risk management information to all sectors of the insurance industry as well as such services as employment prescreening, drug screening, laboratory testing, public records information, and computer software systems.

> EQUIFAX
> 1600 Peachtree Street, N.W.
> Atlanta, GA 30309
> Contact: Norman Black 404-888-5040

GENERAL INSTRUMENT
Announced: 1/7/97

On January 7, 1997, General Instrument (NYSE: GIC) announced a comprehensive strategic restructuring plan to separate into three pubic companies to focus on global growth opportunities. General Instrument Corp. will change its name and spin-off two divisions. The restructuring, expected to be completed in the summer of 1997 through a tax-free spin-off to shareholders, was designed primarily to unlock the share value of NextLevel Systems, Inc., the company's core, high-tech communications systems business. The trivestiture will also create new firms called CommonScope Inc., out of a world-leading coaxial cable manufacturing business, and General Semiconductor Inc., out of electronic component manufacturing operations. GIC's stock closed at $23 1/4, up a half after the announcement.

The new, Chicago-based company will be called NextLevel Systems Inc. and will comprise General Instrument's cable, satellite, and telephone businesses, which had 1996 sales of more than $1.7 billion and employ about

8,300 people worldwide. One spin-off will be called CommScope Inc., comprising the portion of General Instrument than sells coaxial and other electronic cable products. CommScope will be headquartered in Hickory, North Carolina, and has sales of about $560 million. The other spin-off will be General Semiconductor Inc., which had sales of $360 million last year, 70 percent of them outside the United States. Based in Melville, New York, it employs 3,000 people and makes semiconductor products with no direct connection to television or telecommunications.

Reasons for Restructuring

General Instrument's management concluded that the three diverse businesses would be best positioned as independent, public companies. The businesses have different dynamics and business cycles, serve different markets and customers, and are subject to different competitive forces. The restructuring will give the management of each business the ability to focus on its own business, markets, customer requirements, and growth opportunities. In addition, management will be able to design equity-based compensation programs that are targeted to its specific business and performance and therefore be better positioned to attract and retain key personnel.

Here in brief are management's reasons for the spin-off.

- Increase shareholder value:
  —Three "pure play" companies easier to value.
- NextLevel Systems' earnings growing faster than sales:
  —Sales growth from new products and expanding markets.
  —Profit margins growing on production efficiencies.
  —Operating income goal to grow 35 to 45% annually.
- Accelerating earnings growth of NextLevel, starting in 1997, is masked by consolidated GI:
  —Digital video and data start to contribute in 1997.

- CommScope growing faster than cable industry:
  —Increasing market share.
  —Entering new markets.
  —Strong cash flows.
- General Semiconductor growth recovering:
  —Increasing demand for electronic functions.
  —Leveraging global distribution and manufacturing scale.
  —Strong cash flow.
- Management stock incentives tied to each company's performance.

Legal, Tax, and Capital Structure Matters

The restructuring plan is subject to the approval of the holders of a majority of shares of General Instrument and the receipt of a ruling from the Internal Revenue Service that the separation is not taxable to the company or its shareholders. General Instrument intends to tailor each new company's capital structure to insure that it will have the financial flexibility to invest the growth of its world leadership businesses.

FIGURE 10–1

General Instrument

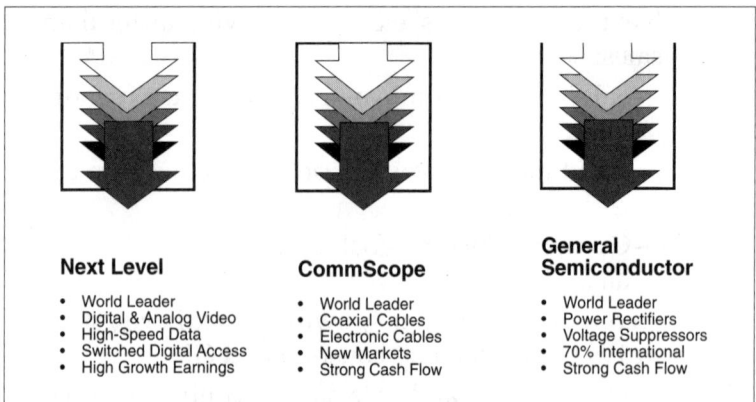

Next Level	CommScope	General Semiconductor
• World Leader	• World Leader	• World Leader
• Digital & Analog Video	• Coaxial Cables	• Power Rectifiers
• High-Speed Data	• Electronic Cables	• Voltage Suppressors
• Switched Digital Access	• New Markets	• 70% International
• High Growth Earnings	• Strong Cash Flow	• Strong Cash Flow

As of December 31, 1996, GI's total debt outstanding was $703 million, of which $228 million are notes convertible into GI's common stock at a conversion price of $23 ¾ per share. General Instrument expects the convertible notes to be converted prior to the spin-offs. Most of General Instrument's debt will loaded onto CommScope and General Semiconductor.

CommScope

CommScope is the world's largest manufacturer of coaxial cables for television systems, with more than 50% market share. CommScope also supplies fiber optic and other high-performance electronic cables. CommScope's cables are used in cable and satellite television networks, telephone networks, local area networks, wireless transmission systems, residential wiring, and airplanes. The company's sales have grown at a compound annual growth rate of approximately 18% since 1993 by increasing market share and focusing on new, high-growth markets, such as international cable television systems, local area networks, and residential wiring. In 1996, approximately 35% of CommScope's sales were outside the United States.

As an established, high-volume manufacturer and distributor with moderate capital expenditures and low R&D requirements, CommScope is a strong cash flow business. Frank Drendel, who has managed the company since 1972, will be the Chairman and CEO of CommScope following its spin-off from General Instrument. The company hopes to grow sales at a CAGR of 18 to 20%, and achieve 16 to 17% operating margins.

General Semiconductor

Power Semiconductor, which will become General Semiconductor, is the world's leading supplier of low-to-medium power rectifiers and transient voltage suppressers used in electronic circuits by automotive, computer, consumer, industrial, and telecommunications manufacturers. Power rectifiers convert alternating current to the direct current used to power electronic circuits. Transient voltage suppressers protect integrated circuits from power surges.

General Semiconductor has a 35-year history of world-class performance based on its high-quality products and strong customer relationships. The company's three-year goal of 14 to 16% annual sales growth is consistent with General Semiconductor's annual growth rate for 1991 to 1994. General Semiconductor generates strong cash flow as a result of operating efficiencies. Future growth should be driven by the demand for increased electronic functions and the company's strong position as a global supplier of high-quality, reliable components. In 1996, approximately 70 percent of sales were outside the United States.

Ronald Ostertag, who has managed the business since 1990, will be the CEO of General Semiconductor following the General Instrument spin-offs. General Semiconductor will be based in Melville, New York, and have approximately 3,300 employees worldwide.

NextLevel Systems

NextLevel Systems will consist of businesses that generated 1996 sales in excess of $1.7 billion as the leading worldwide supplier of systems and components for high-performance networks delivering video, voice, and Internet/data services.

Focus on High-Growth Markets

NextLevel Systems intends to expand beyond its historical cable and satellite television markets by building a major presence in high-growth markets for high-speed data and switched digital access telephone systems. This expansion leverages NextLevel's broad base of core technologies by providing systems and components for the full spectrum of video, voice, and data networks. NextLevel expects its revenue to be more evenly distributed across the cable, satellite, high-speed data, and telephone network markets by the year 2000.

One of NextLevel Systems' goals is substantial profit-margin growth during this period as next-generation products become substantial contributors to earnings. The company expects to derive profit-margin growth from production efficiencies and cost reductions on digital and advanced analog systems, from returns on its investments in digital cable and satellite products (starting in 1997), and from returns on its investment in the NLevel switched digital access telephone system (starting in 1998).

GENERAL INSTRUMENTS
8770 West Bryn Mawr Avenue
Suite #1300
Chicago, IL 60631
Contact: Dick Badler 773-695-1030

GRANCARE
Announced: 9/4/96

GranCare Inc. (NYSE: GC) and Vitalink Pharmacy Services, Inc. (NASDAQ: VTLK), an 82%-owned subsidiary of Manor Care (NYSE: MNR), announced a merger of equals: GranCare's institutional pharmacy business, TeamCare, and Vitalink. The first step in the transaction calls for GranCare to spin-off its skilled nursing operations (New GranCare) in a tax-free distribution to shareholders. The merger will make Vitalink the second largest publicly traded institutional pharmacy company, with revenues of about $400 million. Team Care, a subsidiary of GranCare, provides institutional pharmacy services to over 114,000 customers in 23 states. TeamCare's net revenues for the 12-month period ended May 31, 1996 were $220 million. The merger should generate significant operating savings through purchasing leverage and the elimination of duplicate functions. Vitalink had net revenues of $141 million and net income of $13.9.

Each GranCare shareholder will receive one share of New GranCare common stock and 0.478 of a share Vitalink common stock. New GranCare will trade on the NYSE under the symbol GC. GranCare, Inc., headquartered in Atlanta, is a leading provider of specialty medical services and long-term care. The company operates 140 skilled nursing,

assisted living, and subacute facilities, with over 17,500 beds
in 15 states; 12 home health agencies in 4 states; and, through
its Cornerstone subsidiary, manages 145 specialty programs
in acute care hospitals in 20 states.

> GRANCARE
> One Ravinia Drive #1500
> Atlanta, GA 30346
> Contact: Kay L. Brown 770-393-0199

GENERAL MOTORS
Announced: 1/16/96

On January 16, 1997, General Motors (GM) announced it will
spin-off 100% of Hughes Aircraft to shareholders. It also plans
a tax-free merger of Hughes Aircraft with Raytheon (RTN)
immediately after the spin-off.

The spin-off and merger have a total value of $9.5 bil-
lion to GM and its common stockholders at current stock
prices. The transactions are designed to unlock shareholder
value. General Motors (NYSE: GM) unveiled a series of related transactions designed to address strategic challenges
and unlock shareholder value in its defense electronics, automotive electronics, and telecommunications and space business sectors. GM chairman, chief executive officer, and
president John F. Smith, Jr., announced the following series
of transactions:

■ The tax-free spin-off of 100% of Hughes Aircraft Company to holders of GM's $1-2/3 par value and Class H com-
mon stocks in a distribution ratio to be determined at a later
date. Hughes Aircraft is the defense electronics subsidiary of
GM's Hughes Electronics Corp. (NYSE: GMH). Hughes Aircraft will incur approximately $3.7 to $4.7 billion of new debt
immediately before the spin-off; the proceeds will be used
principally to fund the telecommunications and space business of Hughes Electronics, which will remain a part of GM.

■ The tax-free merger of Hughes Aircraft Company with
Raytheon Company (NYSE: RTN) immediately after the spin-
off. The spin-off and merger have an indicated total value of

$9.5 billion to GM and its common stockholders at current stock prices. That value consists of a combination of approximately $4.7 billion of total debt obligations of Hughes Aircraft at the time of the merger, and $4.8 billion of indicated value of Hughes Aircraft stock to be distributed to common stockholders (after giving effect to the merger and based on Raytheon common stock on the New York Stock Exchange of $47.00 per share). The common stock of Hughes Aircraft to be distributed in the spin-off to GM common stockholders would represent approximately 30% of the stock of the combined company.

■ The transfer of Delco Electronics from Hughes Electronics to GM's Delphi Automotive Systems. At the same time, the 25% derivative interest in the earnings of Delco Electronics currently held by Class H common stockholders will be allocated to holders of GM $1-2/3 common stock in connection with the recapitalization of GM Class H common stock (as described below).

■ The recapitalization of GM's Class H common stock into a tracking stock linked solely to the telecommunications and space business of Hughes Electronics. Currently, GM's Class H common stock tracks the performance of all three Hughes Electronics businesses, namely defense electronics, automotive electronics, and telecommunications.

The company is strategically realigning itself to strengthen its leadership position in a couple of key areas—specifically, telecommunications and space and automotive components. Stockholders will receive direct and immediate value from the spin-off and merger of Hughes' defense operations; in addition, Hughes Electronics will be well positioned to take advantage of emerging opportunities in the telecommunications business, with additional capital available to implement its growth plans. The new Class H common stock will give investors a more focused investment in this business.

GM's automotive components business will be integrated into Delco Electronics. The integration of these businesses will allow GM to create a new category of electronically enhanced vehicle systems with improved functionality, lower cost, and higher quality, and significantly accelerate the newly combined unit's ability to compete more aggressively in high-growth markets worldwide. Combining these units will facilitate the integration of Delco with certain parts of Delphi into a distinct business unit, giving GM the flexibility to consider some form of future partial public ownership of the resulting entity.

The indicated value of the Hughes Aircraft stock to be distributed to GM stockholders would be $5.1 billion, and the corresponding amount of Hughes Aircraft's total debt would be $4.4 billion. In the election of directors to the Raytheon/Hughes Aircraft board, Class A common stock will have an 80.1% voting interest and Class B common stock will have a 19.9% voting interest. Each class will vote separately as to all other matters. Except as to voting rights, the Class A and Class B stock will have identical rights.

The voting difference between the classes reflects a transaction structure that GM believes will allow the spin-off and merger to be tax-free to GM and its stockholders. GM will seek rulings from the U.S. Internal Revenue Service regarding the tax-free nature of the spin-off. The merger transaction is also intended to be tax-free to both GM and Raytheon and their stockholders. Currently, holders of GM Class H have approximately a 25% derivative interest in the earnings of Hughes Electronics; holders of GM $1-2/3 common stock have an approximately 75% derivative interest. In the spin-off, holders of GM $1-2/3 and GM Class H common stocks would collectively receive direct ownership of 100% of the Class A common stock. Holders of GM Class H common stock would receive a distribution of Class A common stock having a value commensurate with their current 25 percent derivative interest in the earnings of Hughes Aircraft, plus an additional amount of this stock to reflect, among other things, the elimination of their 25% derivative interest in the earnings of Delco Electronics. Similarly, the amount of Class A common stock to be distributed to GM's $1-2/3 common stockholders would be less than their current 75 percent interest in order to reflect the net effect of their increased interest in the earnings of Delco Electronics and other elements of the transactions.

The allocation of Hughes Aircraft common stock between the holders of GM's $1-2/3 and Class H common stocks
in the spin-off (the "distribution ratio") will be determined
by the GM Board shortly before soliciting approval of the
transactions from GM $1-2/3 and Class H common stock-
holders. GM expects to solicit stockholder approval in mid-
1997, after certain other conditions are satisfied. The terms of
the entire series of transactions were reviewed by the Capital Stock Committee of the GM Board of Directors, which
recommended the transactions to the Board. The GM Board
has reviewed and approved the transactions, subject to the
determination of a distribution ratio.

GENERAL MOTORS
3044 W. Grand Blvd.
Detroit, MI 48202
Investor Relations 313-556-5000

GULFMARK
Announced: 12/5/96

GulfMark International, Inc. (GMRK) announced plans to
distribute to its stockholders, in a tax-free spin-off, all of the
shares of stock of a new, publicly traded company which will
acquire all of the assets of GulfMark used in connection with
its marine transportation services business. The company
believes that the spin-off will serve to focus attention on the
Company's rapidly growing international offshore marine
activities and thus enhance its ability to access capital to further develop its growth plans.

GulfMark International provides offshore marine services in the international oil and gas markets. The company's
offshore support vessels provide transportation of materials, supplies, and personnel to and from offshore drilling platforms and rigs, production platforms, and other installations.
GulfMark has a fleet of 29 offshore supply vessels operating
in the North Sea and Southeast Asia.

Following the spin-off, the assets of GulfMark will

consist of GulfMark's erosion control services business, approximately 2.2 million shares of Energy Ventures common stock, and certain corporate and miscellaneous assets. In conjunction with the spin-off, GulfMark has entered into a definitive agreement with Energy Ventures, Inc. (NYSE: EVI) pursuant to which Energy Ventures stock will be issued to the stockholders of GulfMark. In the merger, GulfMark stockholders will receive .6695 shares of Energy Ventures common stock for each .share of GulfMark common stock held by such stockholders.

> GULFMARK INTERNATIONAL
> 5 Post Oak Park #1170
> Houston, TX 77027-3414
> Contact: Frank R. Pierce 713-963-9522

ITT HARTFORD
Announced: 2/10/97

ITT Hartford (NSYE: HIG), spun off from ITT Corp. recently, is now splitting off a piece of itself, seeking to raise $900 million by selling a stake in its wholly owned subsidiary, Hartford Life Inc., through an initial public offering. Hartford Life filed a registration statement with the Securities and Exchange Commission to offer as much as 20% of its common stock to the public.

Hartford Life is a provider of investment products, such as annuities, mutual funds, and pension products for savings and retirement, individual, and group life insurance. Hartford Life, with assets of $80 billion as of year-end 1996, is the nation's eighth-largest life insurance group. As of December 31, 1996, The Hartford had assets of $108.8 billion and shareholder equity of $4.5 billion. The offering will provide the unit with capital to expand its operations. News of the offering lifted ITT Hartford's shares $3.125, or 4%, to $78.375. Management believes that the offering will enhance shareholder value by recognizing the market value of the life operations and strengthening the company's financial position.

THE HARTFORD
Hartford Plaza
Hartford, CT 06115
Contact: Stephen Minihan 860-547-2403

LYNCH CORP.
Announced: 12/5/96

Lynch (AMEX: LGL) announced that it is considering the possibility of splitting, through a spin-off, either its multimedia or manufacturing operations. The company said a spin-off would improve management focus, facilitate and enhance financings, and prepare the company for future growth, including acquisitions. LGL feels a split would also help realize the company's underlying values.

Lynch is a diversified manufacturer and provider of multimedia services. Its manufacturing operations comprise Spinaker Industries, Inc. (NASDAQ: SPNI), Lynch Machinery, Inc., and M-tron Industries, Inc. Spinaker, through its two wholly owned subsidiaries, Central Products Company and Brownbridge Industries, Inc., manufacturers adhesive-backed materials. The company manufactures glass-forming machines that are used to produce large television-picture tubes. Lynch's multimedia operations include telephone, personal communication services, cellular, broadcast television, and direct TV and cable TV interests.

The company is controlled by investment manager Mario Gabelli, who is chairman and CEO.

LYNCH CORP.
Eight Sound Shore Dr.
Greenwich, CT 06830
Contact: Mario Gabelli 203-629-3333

MONSANTO
Announced: 12/9/96

Monsanto announced plans to spin-off its chemicals business to focus on agricultural products and biotechnology, shedding 1,500 to 2,500 jobs, or 9% of its workforce. Monsanto said in October it was considering several options, including a restructuring, spin-off, or sale. Chemicals accounted for $3.7 billion or 41% of Monsanto revenue last year. The unit produces nylon carpet fiber, Saflex plastic for windshields and other glass, and specialty chemicals, resins, and coatings. The remainder of Monsanto would be a life sciences company with core businesses of agricultural chemicals, such as its flagship Roundup herbicide, biotech operations, and the G.D. Searle pharmaceutical unit. Its products include herbicides, pesticides, food additives, synthetic sweetener, and Simplesse brand fat substitute. Analysts have speculated that shedding the chemical operations, which are profitable, would enable Monsanto's life sciences business to trade at a higher multiple.

The spin-off is subject to shareowner approval and certain governmental approvals, including a ruling by the U. S. Internal Revenue Service that allows the transaction to be accomplished on a tax-free basis. If shareholders approve the spin-off, they will then receive pro rata shares in the chemical company in a special dividend. These shares will be in addition to those they now hold in Monsanto. The company intends to complete the spin-off no later than the end of 1997. Until the spin-off is complete, the two organizations will operate within Monsanto, beginning early in 1997.

Life Sciences

The life sciences company is built on products that serve the needs of the agriculture, food, and healthcare markets. These include Roundup herbicide, the world's best-selling agricultural product for weed control; Bollgard insect-protected cotton and Roundup Ready soybeans, the leading products in the first-wave of plant biotechnology; NutraSweet brand sweetener, used in thousands of food and beverage products; Ambien, the best-selling prescription drug for the short-term treatment of insomnia; and Daypro and Arthrotec, two leading treatments for arthritis. In 1995, the businesses that now comprise the life sciences company generated approximately $700 million in operating income on sales of $5.3 billion.

Chemicals

The chemical businesses are proven competitors that hold the first or second position in many of their key markets. Among the individual products are nylon and acrylic fibers, including fiber for wear-dated carpets and upholstery; Saflex plastic interlayer for automotive and architectural glass; and phosphorus-based compounds used in specialty intermediates and personal care, industrial and institutional products. The chemical businesses also make and market specialty products, such as ingredients for coatings and adhesives; polymer modifiers, process chemicals, and water treatment chemicals; and functional products, such as Therminol heat transfer fluids, Phos-Chek fire retardants, and Skydrol aviation hydraulic fluids. In 1995, the current chemical businesses generated roughly $285 million in operating income on sales of $2.7 billion, with 40% of its sales outside the United States. The new chemical company will be led by Robert G. Potter as chairman and chief executive officer.

> MONSANTO
> 800 N. Lindbergh Boulevard
> St. Louis, Missouri
> Contact: Scarlett Lee Foster 314-694-2883

PEPSICO
Announced: 1/23/97

PepsiCo Inc. decided it would concentrate on its two strongest businesses—soft drinks and snack foods—and spin-off its restaurant division as an independent, publicly traded company. PepsiCo owns Pizza Hut, Taco Bell, and KFC chains, which together have 29,000 units worldwide, including franchisees. Its $20 billion in annual sales ranks it second to McDonald's in terms of revenue. The spin-off is expected to take the form of a tax-free distribution of the shares of the new company, to be completed by the end of the year. PepsiCo does not plan to assign any of its existing debt to the new company. Following the spin-off, PepsiCo will be the largest U.S. packaged-goods company and will consist of two core businesses: Frito-Lay Co., the world's largest maker of salty snacks; and Pepsi-Cola Co., the world's largest beverage company.

PepsiCo was the most heavily traded issue on the NYSE as bidders pushed the stock up $3.50 to $35.50 the day the spin-off was announced. Rumors of a restructuring have been rampant since last fall, as the price of the stock has significantly trailed the S&P and Coca-Cola. Since year-end 1995, the stock had risen only 18% through the day before the spin-off announcement, versus 28% for the S&P 500 and 60% for Coca-Cola. In making the announcement, PepsiCo's Chairman and Chief executive officer, Roger A. Enrico, said, "Our goal in taking these steps is to dramatically sharpen PepsiCo's focus. Our restaurant business has tremendous financial strength and a very bright future. However, given the distinctly different dynamics of restaurants and packaged goods, we believe all our businesses can better flourish with two separate, distinct managements and corporate structures."

Pepsi has been in the restaurant business since 1977, when it bought Pizza Hut. Taco Bell was added in 1978, and KFC in 1986. Competition in the U.S. restaurant industry, in the form of value pricing to build traffic, has hurt profitability. While Pepsi's restaurant revenue of $11.3 billion in 1995 (excluding franchisees) exceeded that of its soft-drink division, at $10.5 billion, the steep costs of the restaurant operations have been a drag on PepsiCo's earnings. The restaurant business accounted for 37% of PepsiCo's revenue in 1995, but only 24% of its profit.

Following the spin-off of its restaurants, PepsiCo, Inc. will rank as one of the largest packaged goods companies in the United States. For 1996, PepsiCo is expected to post worldwide snack and beverage sales of more than $20 billion. In the United States, PepsiCo's soft-drink volume growth has compounded at 4% annually over the last decade. PepsiCo's

U.S. snack volume has compounded at about 8% per year over the last 10 years and accounts for eight of the top 10 snack-chip brands in American supermarkets. Pepsi will be left with domestic beverages such as Mountain Dew, Slice, Pepsi, Mug Root Beer, All Sport, and Lipton teas. Snack foods include Frito's, Lay's Potato Chips, Baked Lay's, Chee-tos, Ruffles, Rold Gold, Doritos, Tostitos, Funyuns, and Sanitas.

PEPSICO, INC.
700 Anderson Hill Road
Purchase, NY 10577
Contact: Margaret Moore 914-253-2711

PROVIDIAN

Announced: 12/30/96

Louisville-based Providian Corporation (NYSE: PVN) announced it had approved a merger of its insurance operations with AEGON USA in a transaction valued at $3.5 Billion. The deal includes a tax-free exchange of stock of AEGON N.V. shares. In addition to the merger, the company will spin-off Providian Bancorp to shareholders, who will receive one Providian Bancorp share per Providian share and AEGON common shares with a value of $28 per Providian share. Management believes the tax-free restructure provides benefits to shareholders in light of the low tax basis of the individual businesses. The merger of Providian's insurance businesses with AEGON is conditional upon several events, including shareholder approval and various regulatory approvals.

Providian Corporation, with $27.3 billion in assets, is a provider of consumer financial services including insurance and consumer loan, annuity, and pension products. Providian Bancorp will become a separate, publicly traded company utilizing the Providian name. Bancorp offers credit cards, consumer loans, deposit products, and other consumer banking services nationwide. The company has more than $9 billion in managed loans. Headquartered in San Francisco, Providian Bancorp's subsidiaries are First Deposit National

Bank of Tilton, New Hampshire; Providian National Bank in Concord, New Hampshire; and Providian Credit Services, Inc. in Salt Lake City, Utah.

PROVIDIAN
400 West Market Street
Louisville, KY 40232
Contact: Bonnie Otto 502-560-3019

RALSTON PURINA
Announced: 3/29/96

On March 29, 1996, Ralston announced their intention to separate the international agricultural animal feeds business in a tax-free spin-off to shareholders. Completion of the spin-off is contingent upon a favorable tax ruling from the Internal Revenue Service and approval by the Ralston Purina Board of Directors. Assuming satisfactory resolution of these items, the transaction should be completed during 1997.

Ralston Purina Company was founded in 1894. Today it is the world's largest producer of dry dog and soft-moist cat foods, which are marketed under the Purina brand name; the world's largest manufacturer of dry-cell battery products, including Eveready and Energizer brand products; and a major producer of dietary soy protein, fiber food ingredients, polymer products and, outside the United States, of feeds for livestock and poultry. In recent years, Ralston Purina Company has undergone a significant transformation from a widespread conglomerate to a narrow portfolio of global businesses. Guided by an objective to build shareholder value, the company has shed underperforming assets and entered new industries or complemented existing operations through acquisitions. The company now consists of four businesses in global industries.

Management feels legal separation is appropriate because its relationship with Ralston does not generate the level of benefits seen with the other Ralston businesses. Agriculture competes in an industry with extreme local market condition variations and more confined opportunity for technological differentiation. As a result, management expects that the AG business will pursue its objectives more successfully as an independent company.

RALSTON PURINA
Checkerboard Square
St. Louis, MO 63164
Contact: Michael Grabel 314-982-3000

RETIREMENT CARE ASSOCIATES
Announced: 8/1/96

Retirement Care (NYSE: RCA), an owner/operator of retirement facilities and nursing homes primarily in the southeast, has engaged a financial advisor for the spin-off of its assisted living business. NatWest Markets will advise and assist the company in connection with a proposed spin-off of its retirement and assisted living business to Retirement Care's existing shareholders.

Retirement care operates 34 retirement care and assisted living facilities with an approximate resident capacity of 3,700 in eight states. RCA believes that a spin-off will increase shareholder value by better realizing the market value of the retirement and assisted living businesses. RCA owns or operates 95 nursing homes, retirement centers, and assisted living facilities with a total of more than 9,900 beds/units. The facilities are primarily located in Georgia, Florida, Alabama, Tennessee, South Carolina, North Carolina, and Virginia.

RETIREMENT CARE ASSOCIATES
6000 Lake Forrest Dr. #20
Atlanta, GA 30328
Contact: Chris Brogdon 404-255-7500

SANTA FE ENERGY RESOURCES
Announced: 9/18/96

Santa Fe Energy Resources, Inc. (NYSE: SFR) announced a restructuring and public offering of Monterey Resources Subsidiary. On November 20, 1996, the Houston-based company carved out Monterey Resources (NYSE: MRC) in an IPO priced at $14.50 a share that yielded proceeds of about $126 million from the sale of 9.3 million shares. The IPO proceeds were used to pay off about $90 million of indebtedness, and the balance will be used for other corporate purposes. The IPO shares represent approximately 17% of Monterey's outstanding common stock. Santa Fe will continue to own the remaining 83% of Monterey Resources but intends to distribute those shares to holders of SFR common stock in a tax-free spin-off in mid-1997, subject to a favorable ruling from the IRS, consent of SFR's shareholders, and final approval by the SFR Board of Directors. SFR does not expect the spin-off to occur until late in the second quarter of 1997. Santa Fe Energy Resources has indicated it is taking these actions because the operations of the company have developed into two distinctly separate businesses with diverging capital needs and risk profiles. These transactions are designed to allow each business to more efficiently develop its distinct resource base, pursue business opportunities, and provide improved access to capital markets.

Monterey Resources, based in Bakersfield, California, will assume substantially all the assets and liabilities of the Western Division of SFR, which operates primarily in the San Joaquin Valley of California. The Western Division owns and operates properties in the Midway Sunset, Kern River, and South Belridge fields, the three largest producing oilfields in the 48 contiguous states, and is the leading producer in Midway Sunset, the largest of the three fields.

Santa Fe Energy Resources is an independent oil and gas exploration and production company. It has production in the United States, Argentina, and Indonesia, with additional exploration activities in other regions of the world.

SANTA FE ENERGY RESOURCES
1616 S. Voss #1000
Houston, TX 77057
Contact: Kathy E. Hager 713-507-5000

SUMMIT TECHNOLOGY
Announced 1/30/97

On January 30, 1997, Summit Technology (BEAM) announced its intention to divest through sale or spin-off its growing but unprofitable Vision Center clinic business to concentrate on its core opthalic laser systems operations. Summit Technology develops and manufactures ophthalmic laser systems designed to correct refractive-vision disorders, such as near-sightedness, farsightedness, and astigmatism. Its stock jumped 6% to close at $7.813, up 43.75 cents, on NASDAQ. The company's Homium Laser System has been cleared by the U.S. Food and Drug Administration (USFDA) for commercial sale in the United States to treat the symptoms of glaucoma. Its excimer system has been cleared by the USFDA to treat nearsightedness.

Founded in 1985, Summit Technology is a leading developer and manufacturer of ophthalmic laser systems designed to correct common vision disorders. In 1995, Summit was the first excimer laser company to receive FDA approval for its Apex excimer laser system for the correction of mild to moderate myopia in the United States. In addition, through its wholly owned subsidiary, Lens Express, Summit sells contact lenses and related products.

Summit made a change in management in Fall 1996 in an effort to address their lack of profitability. While the new management was excited about the growth and prospects for the Vision Center business, they did not want to alienate customers (primarily physicians who buy the $500,000 equipment) by competing directly with them. In addition, by concentrating on the core laser systems operations, they are more likely to make the company profitable. The company has 220 systems installed in the United States and 220 systems installed outside the United States. The company gets additional fees for each procedure performed by its equipment within the United States. While the market for PRK has not ramped up as fast as people expected, there is potentially a huge market in correcting nearsightedness with lasers.

The company is pursuing FDA approval of its Apex Plus laser system for LASIK and for the treatment of high myopia, astigmatism, and hyperopia. The Apex Plus system represents leading-edge technology and is widely used outside America for these applications.

> SUMMIT TECHNOLOGY
> 21 Hickory Drive
> Waltham, MA 02154
> Contact: Paula L. Elliott 617 672-0517

TRIARC

Announced: 10/29/96

Triarc (NYSE: TRY) on October 29, 1996 announced a plan to offer up to approximately 20% of the shares of its beverage and restaurant businesses to the public through an initial public offering and to spin-off the remainder of the shares of such businesses to Triarc's stockholders. Consummation of the initial public offering and spin-off will be subject to receipt of a favorable ruling from the Internal Revenue Service that the spin-off will be tax-free to the company and its stockholders. The initial public offering and spin-off are not expected to occur prior to the second quarter of 1997.

After the spin-off, Triarc stockholders will own shares in two separate, publicly traded companies: Triarc Companies, Inc. and a consumer products company consisting of the beverage and restaurant businesses. Triarc Companies will then be comprised of National Propane Corporation (Triarc has an approximate 44% interest in National Propane Partners, L.P.) and C.H. Patrick (dyes and specialty chemicals). Triarc will also have approximately $200 million in cash. The new consumer products company will be comprised of the Triarc Restaurant Group (Arby's, Inc., p.t.Noodle's, T.J. Cinnamons, and ZuZu brands) and the Triarc Beverage Group (Royal Crown Company, Inc. and Mystic Brands, Inc.). Management wishes to expand the restaurant and beverage businesses by developing the existing brands and acquiring and developing additional product lines. The spin-off should enhance the beverage and restaurant company's ability to raise capital needed to fund the planned expansion. In addition, it will allow its key people to directly participate in its growth through equity ownership in the business. The restaurant and beverage businesses produce soft-drink concentrates and nonalcoholic beverages and operate fast-food franchises. Royal Crown makes concentrates for RC Cola, Diet Rite Cola, Nehi, and Upper 10 soft drinks. Triarc also makes fruit drinks, ready-to-drink iced teas, and sparkling waters that are sold under the Mistic and Royal Mistic brand names. The company also operates and manages Arby's restaurants and franchises.

Triarc Beverage Group will be headquartered in White Plains, New York. Royal Crown Mistic will continue to operate independent sales and marketing organizations to serve their different distribution systems and marketplace needs. The finance, administration, and operating functions will be consolidated to maximize efficiencies. Triarc closed 1996 at $11 ½.

TRIARC
900 Third Avenue
New York, NY 10022
Contact: Martin M. Shea 212-230-3030

VALERO ENERGY
Announced: 1/31/97

Valero Energy Corporation (NYSE: VLO) is a diversified energy company engaged in the production, transportation, and marketing of specialized petroleum products. The company's core businesses are specialized refining and natural gas related services. On January 31, Valero announced that PG&E

(NYSE: PCG) has been selected to merge with Valero and acquire its natural gas services business, Valero Natural Gas Company, which operates a 7,500-mile natural gas services pipeline system and eight natural gas processing plants in Texas. The acquisition will not include Valero's wholly owned subsidiary, Valero Refining and Marketing Company, which will be spun off prior to the merger.

Based in San Antonio, Texas, Valero Natural Gas Company's operations include the gathering, transportation, marketing, and storage of natural gas; the processing, transportation, and marketing of natural gas liquids; and the marketing of electric power. Valero's subsidiary, Valero Refining and Marketing, refines high-sulfur atmospheric residual oil into premium products, primarily reformulated gasoline, at its 171,500-barrel-per-day refinery in Corpus Christi, Texas, and markets those products.

Each Valero shareholder will receive approximately .63 shares of PG&E common stock for each Valero share, based on a PG&E closing price on January 31, 1997, of $22.75 per share. The value to Valero shareholders is approximately $14.25 per share of Valero stock. Valero's shareholders will also receive one share of the spun-off refining and marketing company. The new refining and marketing company will retain the Valero name and will apply to be listed on the New York Stock Exchange. Both the spin-off of the refining and marketing business and the merger with a subsidiary of PG&E Corporation are expected to be tax-free transactions for Valero shareholders. The merger is expected to be completed by mid-1997.

Management believes that the merger and spin-off of the refining and marketing operations will serve to enhance shareholder value by more fully reflecting the value of each of the two core businesses.

VALERO ENERGY
PO Box 500
San Antonio, TX 78292
Contact: Keith Booke 210-246-2099

WABAN
Announced: 10/23/96

On October 23, 1996, Waban jumped $3 ⅜, to $27 ¼, following news the home-improvement retailer's board approved a plan to spin-off its BJ's Wholesale Club unit in the form of a special dividend to shareholders. The plan would separate BJ's Wholesale chain from its struggling HomeBase division in a bid to raise shareholder value by isolating BJ's higher growth prospects in its own stock. It is likely that BJ's will carry a higher price-to-earnings multiple. In the proposed distribution, stockholders will receive one share in the new BJ's corporation for each Waban share now held. The spin-off is expected to be completed in the spring of 1997. Waban will change its name to HomeBase, Inc. and will continue to operate and develop the home-improvement business.

Waban Inc. currently has two operating divisions: BJ's Wholesale Club and HomeBase. Consolidated net income for the 12-month period ended July 27, 1996 was $75.4 million, or $2.12 per fully diluted share, earned on revenues of $4.2 billion. BJ's Wholesale Club in one of the largest membership warehouse club chains in the northeastern United States, with 79 clubs currently in operation, compared with 68 one year ago. BJ's contributed $95.4 million of operating income to Waban's consolidated financial results in the 12-month period ended July 27, 1996, on sales of $2.7 billion. HomeBase is a merchandiser of home-improvement products in the western United States, currently operating 84 warehouse stores, compared with 79 one year ago. HomeBase contributed $53 million of operating income to Waban's consolidated financial results in the 12-month period ended July 27, 1996, on sales of $1.5 billion.

The Board believes that the spin-off will allow each company's management to focus exclusively on goals appropriate to the further success of its own operations and that the new structure will allow the financial markets to evaluate each business.

WABAN INC.
One Mercer Rd
PO Box 9600
Natick, MA 01760
Contact: Eileen H. Kirrance 508-651-6650

WESTINGHOUSE
Announced: 11/13/96

Westinghouse Electric Corp. (WX) announced it would split
in two, creating a new company from its industrial businesses
to be called Westinghouse Electric Co., or WELCO. The company has moved its emphasis from industry to broadcasting
in recent years. The shift made Westinghouse unwieldy and
hard to value, with little synergy to be realized. The current
parent company will contain the broadcast operations and
move its headquarters to New York City. Its Board of Directors approved a plan to separate its $4.6 billion industrial
business by way of a tax-free spin-off to shareholders, form-
ing the new, publicly traded company, WELCO. It also plans
a public offering by Thermo King of up to 20% of the stock of
Thermo King, its transport temperature control company,
which will become a majority owned subsidiary of WELCO.
The IPO will provide the initial cash funding for WELCO.

It is anticipated that the separation will take place in the
third quarter of 1997, with the planned IPO of Thermo King
taking place prior to the formal spin-off.

Michael Jordan, Chairman and CEO of Westinghouse,
said: "We will create a company with several significant advantages. The new company will focus on two major technologies: transport temperature control and power
generation, including nuclear. Well capitalized and with
strong investment programs for each of its businesses,
WELCO will be a reliable, high-performing supplier to its
customers. With historical obligations now clearly defined
and a rapidly declining cost base, WELCO will be particularly attractive to investors."

The remaining businesses of Westinghouse Electric will
consist of its $4.2 billion broadcasting company, which has

major holdings in radio, television broadcasting and syndication, and cable. The broadcast company will retain all debt obligations of the current Westinghouse Electric Corporation as well as the tax net operating losses (NOL).

The restructuring appears well designed. It creates a pure play media stock (broadcast company), that maximizes the value of the NOL. It launches WELCO with a strong balance sheet and illuminates the value of Thermo King to both the existing shareholders and new investors.

The Broadcast Company

After the spin-off, Westinghouse Electric Corp. (the current parent company) will consist of CBS Inc., the largest television and radio broadcaster, Group W Satellite and distribution company; and Infinity Broadcasting.

WELCO

WELCO will consist of four business units, each with significant market positions and strong technology leadership in its respective industries: Thermo King, Power Generation, Energy Systems, and Government Operations.

Thermo King is the world leader in mobile transport temperature control equipment for trucks and trailers and is a participant in the related markets for bus air-conditioning and seagoing containers.

Westinghouse Power Generation holds market and technology leadership positions for steam and combustion turbines in a global market expected to experience 60% growth in new capacity additions over the next 10 years. Its technology represents 25 percent of the world's installed power generation capacity—the second largest worldwide. Although it faces a difficult domestic market, it maintains a strong position in the high-growth markets of Asia and Latin America that are expected to yield sustained profitable growth.

Westinghouse Energy Systems holds a premier position for nuclear fuel, services, and technology in the $9 billion annual global market.

Westinghouse Government Operations manages Department of Energy sites and Army chemical de-militarization operations, as well as providing development and support services for the Navy's nuclear-powered vessels.

Concurrent with the separation plans, Westinghouse is divesting its Security Systems businesses and restructuring its Pittsburgh corporate headquarters and other industrial businesses to significantly reduce WELCO's overhead and operating costs.

WESTINGHOUSE
11 Stanwix St.
Pittsburgh, PA 15222
Contact: Dave Schields 412-244-2245

ZING TECHNOLOGIES, INC.

Announced: 11/21/96

Zing Technologies (NASDAQ: ZING) reported that its Board of Directors approved in principle the spin-off of all the common stock of its 90%-owned subsidiary, Transitional Analysis of Component Technology, Inc.(TACTech) to shareholders of Zing. June 17, 1997 was the record date for the spin-off.

Zing Technologies is a holding company for Ominrel and TACTech. Omnirel manufactures power hybrid circuits and semiconductor multichip components for military and industrial users. Power hybrid circuits are electronic circuits that regulate the input and output of power to a device. TACTech licenses computer-software databases to military semiconductor manufacturers, the U.S. Department of Defense, and defense contractors. The databases provide information for determining the life cycle of microcircuits.

ZING TECHNOLOGIES
115 Stevens Avenue
Valhalla, NY 10595
Contact: Michelle Mastropolo 914-747-7474

9

Restructuring Revolution: Spin-Off Candidates

I have identified some diversified companies that would benefit from some form of strategic action including a spin-off. This should be a promising avenue of investment, at a time when corporate profit growth is moderating and the market as whole is pretty fully priced. The following is a list of diversified companies that could be candidates for spin-offs.

ALBERTO: CULVER (NYSE: AVC)

Alberto-Culver is best known for its consumer brands, such as Alberto-Culver VO5, Static Guard, Sugartwin, Mrs. Dash, and Molly McButter. But the company also operates about 1,500 Sally Beauty stores, which sell hair-care products, skin-care products, cosmetics, and other beauty items. Sally Beauty is the world's largest chain of stores selling hair-care products at discount prices to people in the salon trade. The shares do not properly reflect the value of this franchise.

ALLIEDSIGNAL (NYSE: ALD)

Many analysts regard AlliedSignal as a classic conglomerate and break-up candidate. The company, with operations in aerospace, automotive parts, and engineered materials, is broadly diversified. Since Chairman Lawrence Bossidy took over in 1991, he has cut payrolls, divested assets, and streamlined operations. As a result, productivity and earnings have shown steady improvement. But much of Bossidy's compensation is tied to the stock's price, and Wall Street would likely applaud a spin-off of a noncore business.

DRESSER INDUSTRIES (NYSE: DI)

Dallas-based Dresser Industries provides products and services to the petroleum industry. Through various acquisitions, Dresser has built up a solid, upstream oilfield business. However, uneven performance as a result of some downstream operations has penalized the stock. The company's stock price would benefit if the downstream businesses were divested.

DU PONT (NYSE: DD)

Du Pont makes chemicals and related products. Its Conoco subsidiary produces petroleum products. This huge oil company, which Du Pont acquired in 1981 at the height of the hard assets mania, is a good example of what is wrong with conglomerate mergers. Conoco is essentially a no-growth business, whereas the chemicals business has a reputation as a leading producer of specialty chemicals.

GANNETT (NYSE: GCI)

Gannett provides news, entertainment, and information services throughout North America. The company publishes over 90 daily newspapers, including *USA Today*. In addition, the company operates TV stations, radio stations, and the largest outdoor-advertising company in North America.

HILLENBRAND (NYSE: HB)

Hillenbrand operates four business segments: healthcare, burial caskets, durables, and insurance. Its funeral-service business includes Batesville Casket, which manufactures caskets, and Forethought Life Insurance, a marketer of funeral-planning insurance. The company's Hill-Rom subsidiary produces hospital beds, stretchers, and other equipment, which it sells to hospitals throughout the U.S. and Canada. HB's other healthcare subsidiaries provide therapy beds and home infusion-therapy products. The company's Medeco subsidiary makes high-security locks and access-control products.

PHILLIP MORRIS (NYSE: MO)

Phillip Morris manufactures tobacco products, food products, and beer. The tobacco division produces cigarettes under brand names such as Marlboro, Virginia Slims, and Merit. The company's Kraft General Foods subsidiary makes food products under many brand names. Miller Brewing makes beer sold under the Miller, Lowenbrau, Meister Brau, Icehouse, Red Dog, and Milwaukee's Best brand names. The tobacco business is a likely spin-off candidate due to persistent litigation issues. Many states are trying to recoup millions in healthcare costs spent on people with illnesses tied to tobacco use. This has weighed heavily on the industry in recent years. American Brands recently announced that they will spin-off their U.K. tobacco business in 1997. Shareholders have been pressuring RJR Nabisco to separate the tobacco division from its food businesses. It is likely that at some point Phillip Morris will do the same.

VARIAN ASSOCIATES (NYSE: VAR)

VAR makes electronic systems and components. It manufactures radiation equipment for cancer therapy and industrial inspections and water-fabrication equipment for the semiconductor industry. In addition, the company makes analytical instruments, vacuum equipment, and leak detectors sold for use in industry and research. The private market value of Varian is higher than current stock prices, judging from the value of its three main businesses: semiconductor equipment, healthcare systems, and instruments. Most likely to be sold or spun-off is semiconductor equipment.

WARNER: LAMBERT (NYSE: WLS)

Warner-Lambert is a diversified manufacture of pharmaceutical, consumer healthcare, and gum and mints products. The company's Parke-Davis and Goedecke pharmaceuticals include therapeutic drugs, vaccine, oral contraceptives, and the Nicotrol transdermal nicotine patch. Warner-Lambert's consumer products include Tetra aquarium products, Schick razors, Rolaids antacids, Halls cough suppressants, and Listerine mouthwash. Its confectionery product line includes Certs breath mints and Sugar Babies candy.

TELEPHONE & DATA SYSTEMS INC. (AMEX: TDS)

Last but not least, I have identified a Chicago-based company called Telephone Data Systems that is in desperate need of several spin-offs. In my opinion, the private market value of TDS is at least twice what the stock currently trades (about $37).

TDS is a very strong candidate for some significant corporate restructuring. The stock is trading at close to a five-year low, incensing high-profile shareholders such as Michael Price and Mario Gabelli. They are pressing the telecommunications company to break apart its three most promising holdings—TDS Telecommunications Corp., U.S. Cellular Corp. and Aerial Communications Inc.—and sell its struggling American Paging Inc. subsidiary.

TDS provides local and cellular phone, paging, and other telecommunication services. TDS Telecommunications, a subsidiary, operates 100 telephone companies, which supply local-telephone service to more than 445,000 access lines in 28 states and also provides custom-calling services. The company's other primary operating subsidiaries include majority-owned United States Cellular (USM), which manages cellular systems with approximately 710,000 customers;

American Paging (APP), an 82%-owned subsidiary which provides paging services to about 785,000 customers; and Aerial Communications (AERL), an 83%-owned subsidiary, TDS's start-up PCS business. United States Cellular is the crown jewel of the TDS portfolio. The company's operating results are very strong.

Small parts of American Paging, U.S. Cellular, and Aerial Communications (a start-up supplier of digital wireless phone services) are publicly traded, but TDS owns more than 80% of each. In addition, the Carlson family (who founded and controls the company) controls 51.5% of holding company voting rights through a special class of stock—essentially super voting power. This is part of the reason the company stock has slumped despite strong operating performance and a raging bull market. Based on the prices of the its publicly traded subsidiaries, at $37, TDS trades at a significant discount to the sum of its parts, which is at a minimum worth $50. Why the disparity? The stock seems to suffer from a Carlson family control discount. TDS (under shareholder pressure) has hired First Boston and Salomon to explore restructuring scenarios.

TDS Telecom provides telephone service to rural and suburban America. The company is an efficient, growing telephone business and is somewhat insulated from competition by its smaller market focus. TDS is an attractive business, given its high profitability, free cash flow, and nonmetropolitan geographic positioning.

United States Cellular is one of the fastest-growing cellular companies in the industry and is substantially insulated from competition by its rural geographic emphasis. The company continues to post superior subscriber growth. USM registered year-over-year internal customer growth of 6% in 1995. The company has been successful in creating clusters of nonmetropolitan cellular properties. Over the past five years the company has almost doubled its managed POPs to 21.5 million in a series of acquisitions.

Aerial Communications is the eighth-largest PCS licensee in the country, with over 27 million POPs. The company's six licenses cover Minneapolis–St.-Paul; Tampa–St. Petersburg–

Orlando; Houston; Pittsburgh; Kansas City; and Columbus, Ohio. These properties fill in and expand the wireless presence TDS has with United States Cellular.

American Paging is engaged in the highly competitive paging business, where margins and pricing are falling. The company has reported disappointing results, with no quick fix in sight. A number of shareholders have supported the idea of selling the unit.

Investors are demanding a change in TDS's capital structure. The stock of three of the company's four subsidiaries trade publicly. However, given the minority ownership stake in each company that investors have, as well as the small float, the companies trade at a discount to comparable publicly traded companies. Many investors have suggested that TDS break up or sell parts of the company to enhance the public market value.

SPIN-OFF/SALE ALTERNATIVES

If shareholders get their way, *American Paging probably will be sold off.* Such a transaction would be viewed favorably by the market.

United States Cellular could be spun-off to shareholders. This would likely provide the most upside potential for shareholders, but probably is not palatable to management.

TDS Telecom could be spun-off to shareholders or partially carved out. The proceeds from a carve-out could be used to finance future telephone company acquisitions. TDS Telecom would be publicly traded, potentially receiving a significant valuation from the market.

Aerial Communications could be spun-off to shareholders, or kept with TDS Telecom under TDS umbrella.

At any rate, I believe the company needs to engage in some significant form of capital restructuring to close the gap between the current market valuation and private market value.

Endnotes

CHAPTER 1

1. For an extensive discussion of the long-term returns of spin-offs, see "Restructuring Through Spin-Off," *Journal of Financial Economics*, 1993, vol. 33, by James A. Miles and J. Randall Woolridge (Pennsylvania State University) and Patrick J. Cusatis (Lehman Brothers).

2. Cusatis, Patrick J., James A. Miles, and J. Randall Woodridge, "Some New Evidence That Spin-Offs Create Value," *Journal of Applied Corporate Finance*, Summer 1994, vol. 7, pp. 100-107.

3. Hite and Owers, "Security Price Reactions Around Corporate Spin-Off Announcements," *Journal of Financial Economics*, 1983, vol. 12(4), pp. 409-436; Shipper and Smith, "Effects of Restructuring on Shareholders Wealth: The Case of Voluntary Spin-Offs," *Journal of Financial Economics*, 1983, vol. 12(4), pp. 437-468; and Miles and Rosenfeld, "The Effect of Voluntary Spin-Off Announcements on Shareholder Wealth," *Journal of Financial Economics*, 1983, vol. 38, pp. 1597-1606—each documents a mean abnormal spin-off announcement return of approximately three percent.

CHAPTER 4

1. See B. Seifert and B. Rubin, "Spin-Offs and the Listing Phenomenon," *Journal of Economics and Business*, 1989, vol. 41.

References

Alexander, G.P., G. Benson, and J. Kampmeyer. "Investigating the Valuation Effects of Announcements of Voluntary Corporate Sell-Offs" 1984, *Journal of Finance*, 39(2): 503-517.

Cusatis, Patrick J., James A. Miles, and J. Randall Woodridge, "Restructuring through Spin-Offs," *Journal of Financial Economics*, 1993, 33(3): 293-311.

Cusatis, Patrick J., James A. Miles, and J. Randall Woodridge, "Some New Evidence That Spin-Offs Create Value," *Journal of Applied Corporate Finance*, 1994, 7 Summer, 100-107.

Hite, Gailen L., and James E. Owers, "Security Price Reactions Around Corporate Spin-Off Announcements," *Journal of Financial Economics*, 1983, 12(4): 409-436.

Michaely, Roni, and Wayne H. Shaw, "The Choice of Going Public: Spin-Offs vs. Carve-Outs," *Financial Management*, 1995, 24(3): 5.

Miles, James, and James Rosenfeld. "The Effect of Voluntary Spin-Off Announcements on Shareholder Wealth," *Journal of Financial Economics*, 1983, 38: 1597-1606.

Schipper, Katherine, and Abbie Smith, "Effects of Restructuring on Shareholders Wealth: The Case of Voluntary Spin-Offs," *Journal of Financial Economics*, 1983, 2(4): 437-468.

Schipper, Katherine, and Abbie Smith, "A Comparison of Equity Carve-Outs and Seasoned Equity Restructurings: Share Price Effects and Corporate Restructuring," *Journal of Financial Economics*, 1986 15: 153-186.

Seifert, Bruce, and Bruce Rubin, "Spin-Offs and the Listing Phenomenon," *Journal of Economics and Business*, 1989, 41.

Slovin, Myron, Marie Sushka, and Steven Ferraro, "A Comparison of the Information Conveyed by Equity Carve-Outs, Spin-Offs, and Asset Sell-Offs," *Journal of Financial Economics*, 1995, 37.

Index

AC Nielson (ART), 94–96
accounting, effect of spin-off on, 31–32
acquisitions:
  as aftermath of spin-off, 9, 19, 20, 34, 51, 79, 131, 133, 140, 143
  spin-off to prevent hostile, 83–84
ACX Technologies (ACTX), 71
administrative services, 21
Adolph Coors Co. (ACCOB), 71
AEGON USA, 173–174
Aerial Communications (AERL), 188–190
aerospace manufacturing, 124–125
agricultural products, 170–171, 174–175
air freight businesses, 126
airline industry, 21, 75–76, 91, 118–119
AirTouch Communications (ATI), 125
Albemarle (ALB), 98–99
Alberto Culver (AVC), 185
Alco Standard Corp. (ASN), 72–73
Allen Group, Inc. (ALN), 7, 73–75
AlliedSignal (ALD), 185–186
allocation issues, effect of spin-off on, 31
Allstate Corp., 9, 21, 134
Alltrista Corp. (JARS), 79
Alumax Inc. (AMX), 88
Ambac Inc., 12, 16
American Biltrite, 12, 15
American Brands (AMB), 149–150
American Express (AXP), 75
American Paging (APP), 188–190
Amerigas Partners, L.P., 11, 12
AMR Corp. (AMR), 75–76
Andrews Group, 20
Anheuser-Busch (BUD), 76–77
Aptar Group, Inc. (ATR), 126
Armour Food Company, 90
Ascent Entertainment Group, Inc. (GOAL), 12, 13
Ascent Network Services, Inc., 13
Ashland Exploration, 150–151
Ashland Inc., 150–151

asset transfers, spin-off role in, 3–4, 6, 33
AT&T Corp. (T), 4, 10–11, 77–79
automotive industry, 7, 30–31, 73–75, 80–81, 138, 139, 165–166
Aviall, Inc. (AVL), 130–131
aviation services, 130–131

Ball Corp. (BLL), 79
Bally Entertainment Corp., 8
Bally Total Fitness, 8–9
banking industry, 84–85, 135, 173–174
Banz, Rolf, 55
Bateville Casket, 186
Bath & Body Works, 12, 17–18
Baxter International (BAX), 79–80
Beacon Communications, 13
Billing Information Concepts (BILL), 142–143
BJ's Wholesale Club, 181–182
Boise Cascade Office Products Corp. (BOP), 12, 13–14
bondholders, views of spin-offs, 62–63
Borders Group, Inc., 21
Bossidy, Lawrence, 185–186
Botson, Ib, 35
brewing industry, 71, 76–77, 187
Briggs & Stratton (BGG), 7, 80–81
broadcasting industry (see Television businesses)
building industry, 11, 12, 15
Burlington Resources (BR), 81

Cadence Design Systems Inc., 12, 16–17
Caliber System, Inc. (CBB), 81–82
capital allocation, spin-off effects on, 34
Capital One Financial Corp. (COF), 135
capital structure, effect of spin-off on, 31
Caremark International (CK), 79–80
CarMax Group, 30–31
carve-outs, 9–20, 20–21

195

home improvement products, 11, 12,
  15, 181
home security businesses, 126
Home Shopping Network (HSN), 111–
  112
HomeBase, Inc., 181–182
Homestake Mining Corp., 131
Hospitality Properties Trust (HPT), 12,
  16
Host Marriott Corp. (HMT), 7, 112–113
Host Marriott Services (HMS), 7, 112–
  113
hotel industry, 7, 12, 16, 112–113, 117,
  120–121
H&R Block (HRB), 103–105
Hughes Aircraft Co., 164–167
Hughes Electronics (GMH), 25–26, 165
Humana Inc. (HUM), 113

Icahn, Carl, 133
IKON Office Solutions, 72–73
Imation (IMN), 122–123
Imperial Tobacco (IMTL), 107–109
index funds, effects on spin-offs, 54, 60,
  61
INDRESCO Inc. (ID), 93–94
industrial equipment, 83–84, 85–86
information services, 16, 94–96, 103–
  105, 122–123, 157
information systems, 11, 12, 16, 82–83
initial public offering (IPO):
  and carve-outs, 9
  divestiture type, 20–21
  vs. spin-off, 7, 35, 44
Inland Steel, Inc. (IAD), 113–114
institutional investors:
  and spin-off investment timing, 65
  effect on spin-offs, 53–54, 56
instrumentation industry, 13, 19, 187
insurance industry, 117, 134, 140
  health, 7, 9
  life, 168–169, 173–174
  mortgage, 21
  property and casualty, 105–106
  risk management services, 158
Integrated Measurement Systems, Inc.
  (IMSC), 12, 16–17
Interco, (ISS), 114–115
Internal Revenue Service, tax
  requirements for spin-offs, 4, 48–50

Internet access industry, 103–105, 134,
  162
Intimate Brands, Inc. (IBI), 12, 17–18
investment banking industry, 11, 12,
  15, 75
investors:
  advantages of spin-offs for, 4–6, 33
  spin-offs vs. tracking stocks for, 29–
  31
  and split-off choices, 21–23
  and targeted stock, 26, 27
Investors Financial Services Corp.
  (IFIN), 21, 96–98
ITT Corp. (ITT), 7, 115–117
ITT Hartford (HIG), 7, 115–116, 168–
  169
ITT Industries (IIN), 7, 115–116

James River Corp., 7
Jordan, Michael, 182

Kimberly-Clark (KMB), 7, 21, 117–119
Kmart Corp., 21
Kraft General Foods, 187

Lehman Brothers (LEH), 75
The Limited Inc., 12, 17–18
LIN Broadcasting (LINB), 119–120
LIN Television Corp. (LNTV), 119–120
Litton Industries (LIT), 120
Lucent Technologies (LU), 4, 10–11, 77
luggage products, 131–133
Lynch Corp. (LGL), 169
Lynch Machinery, 169

majority spin-off, 7–8
management:
  and disadvantages of conglomerates, 52
  effect of spin-off on, 31, 34, 50, 57
  and instabilities of spun-off
  companies, 44
Manor Care, Inc. (MNR), 120–121, 163–
  164
Marathon Group (MRO), 26, 28
marine transportation services, 167–
  168
market performance (see Performance,
  market)
marketing information businesses, 94–
  96

Joseph W. Cornell is a principal of High Yield Analytics, Inc., a Chicago based investment boutique that caters to institutional investors. He is a well-known authority on spin-off investing strategies. Cornell holds a B.B.A. and MBA from Loyola University of Chicago.